POETRY RE

A U T U M N   1 9 9 9   V O L U M E

EDITOR PETER FOR

PRODUCTION STEPHEN T

ADVERTISING LISA RO

CONTENTS

Meeting Ted Hughes

ges 3 – 9

Carolyne Wright on her meeting with Ted Hughes in Bangladesh in 1989; Ian Sansom on *The Epic Poise* (10)

The Geoffrey Dearmer Prize

12 – 26

Comment by the judge, Sheenagh Pugh; poems by Sarah Wardle, Angela Leighton (15), Ros Barber (16), Hugh Macpherson (18), V. G. Lee (20), R. G. Binns (22), Cate Parish (25)

Douglas Dunn

27 – 35

interviewed by Attila Dösa

Poems

36 – 55

by James Lasdun, Harry Clifton (41), Carole Satyamurti (43), Kwame Dawes (44), Roberto Mussapi (46), Rita Ann Higgins (47), Peter Bland (49), Peter Redgrove (50), Connie Bensley (51), Robert Saxton (53), Jayanta Mahapatra (54), Fred Voss (55)

The Review Pages

56 – 62

Harry Clifton on the *Harvill Book of Twentieth Century Poetry in English*; Kevan Johnson on Anne Carson (58); Paul Groves on Robert Minhinnick (60); Hugh Macpherson on Finnish poetry (61)

The Sonnet History

63

John Whitworth on J. H. Prynne

Reviews

64 – 71

David Wheatley on Australian poetry; Ian McMillan on Kate Clanchy (66); Gillian Allnutt on Mark Roper, Katie Donovan, Sarah Corbett, Jane Draycott, Jeet Thayil, Donny O' Rourke (67); John Burnside on Don Paterson's translations of Machado (70)

Poems

72 – 82

by John Latham, Diana Hendry (73), K. M. Dersley (74), Atar Hadari (75), Tim Liardet (76), Douglas Houston (77), John Greening (78), Andy Croft (79), Billy Collins (81), Elaine Feinstein (82)

Reviews

83 – 87

Rod Mengham on Paul Muldoon; Keith Jebb on J. H. Prynne (84); Carol Rumens on Ciaran Carson (86)

The Classic Poem

88

Philip Gross on Rilke's Tenth Elegy

Reviews

90 – 94

Jane Holland on Sheenagh Pugh, Sophie Hannah, Tobias Hill and Fergus Allen; Peter Forbes on Faber anthologies of short poems and sonnets (92); Peter Forbes on Wisława Szymborska (93); poem by Penelope Shuttle (94)

Endstops

95-96

News, Comment, Letters

All illustrations by Gerald Mangan

Manchester Poetry Festival
6-14 November 1999

Monday 8th
Sujata Bhatt, Mimi Khalvalti and Peter Sansom
7.30pm, Waterstones, St Anne's Square
£3 (including refreshments and a book token) full disabled access

Thursday 11th
Helen Dunmore, Jamie McKendrick and Sarah Corbett
7.30pm, Waterstones, St Anne's Square
£3 (including refreshments and a book token) full disabled access

Saturday 13th
Simon Armitage – Out of Bounds
7.30pm Whitworth Art Gallery, Oxford Road, tel: 0161 275 7450; full disabled access.

For a copy of this year's Manchester Poetry Festival brochure contact: Manchester Poetry Festival, 2nd Floor, Enterprise House, 15 Whitworth Street West, Manchester M1 5WG

Tel: 0161 907 0031 Fax: 0161 907 0037
Email: mpf@dial.pipex.com or visit the festival website at www.mpf.dnx.co.uk

Receive 10% off the above with the production of this advert.

POETRY REVIEW
SUBSCRIPTIONS
Four issues including postage:

UK individuals £27
Overseas individuals £35
(all overseas delivery is by airmail)
USA individuals $56

Libraries, schools and institutions:
UK £35
Overseas £42
USA $66

Single issue £6.95 + 50p p&p (UK)

Sterling and US dollar payments only. Eurocheques, Visa and Mastercard payments are acceptable.

Bookshop distribution:
Signature
Telephone 0161 834 8767

Design by Philip Lewis
Cover by Stephen Troussٍeé

Typeset by Poetry Review.

Printed by Grillford Ltd at
26 Peverel Drive, Bletchley,
Milton Keynes MK1 1QZ
Telephone: 01908 644123

POETRY REVIEW is the magazine of the Poetry Society. It is published quarterly and issued free to members of the Poetry Society. Poetry Review considers submissions from non-members and members alike. To ensure reply submissions must be accompanied by an SAE or adequate International Reply coupons: Poetry Review accepts no responsibility for contributions that are not reply paid.

Founded 24 February 1909
Charity Commissioners No: 303334
© 1999

EDITORIAL AND BUSINESS ADDRESS:
22 BETTERTON STREET, LONDON WC2H 9BU

telephone   **0171 420 9880**
fax   **0171 240 4818**
email   **poetrysoc@dial.pipex.com**
website   **http://www.poetrysoc.com**

The Poetry Society is supported by

ISBN 1 900771 17 9
ISSN 0032 2156

What Happens in the Heart

CAROLYNE WRIGHT ON AN
ENCOUNTER WITH TED HUGHES

JUST WHEN EVERY literary critic and Sylvia Plath devotee thought that they had sorted out the truth about Plath and her husband Ted Hughes, along came the February 27, 1998, publication of Hughes' *Birthday Letters*, a remarkable sequence of love poems about his and Plath's tumultuous seven-year marriage. In front-page articles on both sides of the Atlantic, critics and poetry lovers speculated as to why Hughes, Britain's Poet Laureate since 1984, had abruptly broken his unrelenting and controversial silence about his life with Plath, 35 years after she laid her head on a gas oven door and committed suicide. Nobody, it seemed, had any idea that Hughes was quietly composing this poetic memoir over the last three decades.

Nobody, that is, except a few close friends and at least one serendipitously encountered individual. In November 1989, Hughes himself had disclosed this extraordinary information to me in a most unlikely place – on a boat cruise on the Buriganga River in Bangladesh. What he was writing would clarify the true nature of his and Plath's relationship, Hughes had told me, and he intended to publish it posthumously. Although he never asked me to keep his revelation confidential, I knew of his reticence about Plath, I deeply respected his implicit trust, and though I startled a few literary friends by mentioning that this conversation had occurred, I never told anyone the substance of it. But I carefully made notes and recorded impressions against the day when the writings to which he had alluded were at last published.

February was a signal month for Hughes – it marked the anniversary both of his first dramatic meeting with Plath in 1956 and of her death in 1963. The initial mystery as to why Hughes decided to publish *Birthday Letters* that February was clarified by the sad fact of his death, after an 18-month struggle against cancer, on 28 October 1998. It was not quite the posthumous publication he had mentioned, but the deeply private Hughes revealed his illness only to friends. Indeed, when I first read in January 1998 about the publication of *Birthday Letters*, in articles in *The New York Times* and elsewhere, and realized that this was the writing Hughes

had told me of in 1989, my first thought was: "How's his health?" (I later learned of his illness, but not of its severity.) One hopes that Hughes was gratified, perhaps even consoled, by the overwhelmingly sympathetic response to the book from all but a few rigidly vitriolic critics. He also lived to see the publication of his and Sylvia's daughter Frieda's own first collection of poems. *Birthday Letters* promises to be one of the century's most compelling memoirs in verse, and we can be glad that Hughes was with us to share its first several months of life.

Ted Hughes had come to Bangladesh as Chief Guest of Honour at the Second Asia Poetry Festival, a Bangladesh government-sponsored event held in Dhaka in November 1989. I was a Fulbright fellow in the second month of what would be a nearly two-year stay in Dhaka, translating the work of Bangladeshi women poets and writers for an anthology in progress; I had already spent two years in Calcutta translating West Bengali women poets and writers. The writers and literary people with whom I worked urged me to attend the festival, preparations for which dominated newspaper headlines and reports on the sole national television channel.

"It will be very prestigious", my new Bangladeshi friends said. "And you will meet the Guest of Honour, that great Asian poet, Ted Hughes". They laughed at their own wit; some of them, uncertain about the g-h-e-s sequence in this English surname, pronounced his name Ted *HUGE-es*. It would have been impolite to correct them, and I enjoyed this rendition too much to want to change it. In the coming months, it became an affectionate allusion: whenever we reminisced about the Asia Poetry Festival, my Bangladeshi friends and I would wonder aloud how "*HUGE-es Saheb*" was doing, or if he had written anything about his visit.

I met Hughes on the first day of the festival, during the mid-morning tea break after the opening session. Across the room, he towered head and shoulders above the clusters of Bangladeshi journalists and the Thai and Indonesian and Bhutanese guest poets resplendent in their national dress. (I could see in him "that big, dark, hunky boy, the only one there huge enough for me", as Plath had called him in her journal entry about their first meeting in February 1956 – "*HUGE-es Saheb*" indeed). Except for a few Soviet poets with blond hair and gray eyes – who counted geographically as Asian but who hovered at the edges of the room, talking among themselves – Hughes was the only other person besides myself of European ethnicity. The famous craggy features were unmistakeable, though the dark hair of his youth had silvered; and the tall, rangy, broad-shouldered figure had filled out, conveying an impression of massive, solid gravitas. In his dark woolen suit, he could have been a former American football player turned professor of English Literature.

Still a bit apprehensive, I hung back, talking with a Dhaka journalist I had met a few weeks earlier; but I thought I glimpsed a flicker of curiosity across the Poet Laureate's face when he noticed me, the Anglo woman in a *sari*, balancing a teacup and chatting with Bengalis in their language. When we were introduced a few minutes later, Hughes turned his attention to me with a warmth and focussed concentration I had not expected. Hearing my American accent, he smiled: "It seems we're the only native English speakers here". He signed my battered copy of *Crow* – which I had brought with me from America though I had had no idea that I would soon meet its author in Dhaka. He asked me to sit with him and his government-provided liaison during the next session, and recount how I had become interested in the Bengali language and its literature.

"You can function here as a real bridge between cultures", he said. He wanted me to explain to him some of the nuances of the Bengali conversations swirling around us, the cultural context within which this poetry festival operated, the qualities of the Bengali women's poetry I was translating.

I was awed and flattered and humbled to think that there was anything I could tell the Poet Laureate of England; but for the duration of the festival, Hughes invited me to join in his activities there, and in the cultural programs and local sightseeing that the government had arranged for his days in Dhaka. Sitting beside him in the Osmany Hall auditorium for the rest of the morning session, exchanging occasional comments and making impromptu translations of Bengali speeches, I felt included in an open literary circle of global extent. Hughes emanated a powerful presence, but his charisma seemed free of affectation – a quiet, self-contained vitality that allayed any uncertainties I may have had about him. He was immensely interested, in a reserved, low-key way, in the exotic cultural efflorescence around him. He did not act like an Eminence; nor was there any trace, in this man in his late fifties, of arrogance or a will to domineer – none of the rough edges or spirited self-absorption of youth. He seemed very much a gentleman, with a thoughtful, deliberate manner: did I also detect a profound sadness, the trace of decades-old psychic wounds? Perhaps I was only projecting from all that I had read about this famous poet-couple, but I could begin to glimpse why the young Sylvia Plath would have been so wildly attracted to the youthful Ted Hughes – to his physical and psychic magnetism, and above all to his profound and genuine kindness. He was someone with whom, I imagined, she sensed she could find not only mutual poetic inspiration and passionate romance, but also psychic shelter from her own terrors and inner demons.

On the final day of the Asia Poetry Festival, Ted Hughes and I stood at the railing of the *Rangapalli*, the launch rented by the organizers for the obligatory *noubihar*, the river cruise to which all guests of honor in Bangladesh are subjected. We talked, resting our elbows on the polished railing in the full sun of a tropical mid-November, leaning into the view before us – the Buriganga River's procession of fishing skiffs and cargo barges with patched sails, hand-adzed scows that groaned to their gunnels with harvested rice or jute stalks, boatmen polling in slow motion upstream to the nearest docking, singing river ballads in mournful modes. The banks of the river were dotted with clusters of banana plants and date palms, faded pastel houses and small mosques, and sandy stretches where groups of village women slapped wet clothes on flat rocks.

In this unlikely setting, we leaned on the railing and talked, in the cordial tones of recently acquainted junior and senior colleagues, of how amazing it was, especially for him, to be here. We talked about accents – how the English spoken in Bangladesh (as a second language, learned in school) was much closer in its pronunciation and intonations to British than to American English, and how his mother had encouraged her children to move away from the West Yorkshire dialect of their youth and learn a more standard speech at school and through the BBC. He noted my American accent, and said that he had become very familiar with American English when he lived for two years in the United States with – and here he hesitated ever so slightly – "with, you know, my late wife. Sylvia".

I almost stopped breathing. He had mentioned her: it was as if he had uttered one of the forbidden names of God. So private was this topic for him – from all that I had read and heard – that he never answered interview questions about her, and never spoke of her with journalists or biographers. But here was the man himself bringing her up, gesturing toward the river as if that would call forth her image in the syllables of her name. What could I say in reply, without trampling on sacred space? As he went on about how the river scene before us might have figured in her poetry, I murmured something neutral, sympathetic, but not as deeply sympathetic as I meant – I didn't want the eagerness and awe I felt to interfere.

"Yes," I said, "she would have found this world quite an experience". And then, rashly:

"It must be (I searched for bland but empathetic adjectives) amazing and strange to dwell in the aftershadow of that life, the events (I couldn't bring myself to say separation or suicide) of the time, and the ongoing attention to her, the legend she's become..." I stopped, afraid that I had already overspoken.

But he was leaning his elbows on the railing, his hands folded, fingers interlaced – a stance for continuing a conversation. "Yes", he nodded, looking out at the figures on the riverbank. "Very much so. But I've avoided all the biographies, the cult that's grown up around her". He then asked if I had seen the recent biography, *Bitter Fame*, by Anne Stevenson. I had not – the book had just begun to appear in stores as I was leaving the U.S. for Bangladesh. (I had read much of Hughes' and Plath's own poetry, as well as A. Alvarez's searing account, in *The Savage God*, of Plath's last days and details of her suicide; Marjorie Perloff's article, in *The American Poetry Review*, which took Hughes severely to task for his editing of the *Ariel* poems; and a memoir essay by Hughes' long-time friend Lucas Myers, which I perused in a literary magazine one afternoon in the late 1980s, and which recounted the Cambridge University days when Plath and Hughes first met. This piece presented nuanced but deeply sympathetic portrayals of both poets. It would also appear as an appendix in the Stevenson book in 1989, but without prior publication credit; despite extensive searches through the various guides to periodical literature, I have been

unable to recall or identify the journal in which I first read it.) Stevenson had been commissioned to write *Bitter Fame*, Hughes said. At first it was to be a monograph, but then it expanded into a much larger volume after she gained access to papers held by Sylvia's mother and brother.

Stevenson had approached him at one point, Hughes continued. He told her that he wouldn't stop her, but he would give no interviews, and would have nothing to do with the writing of the book. Ultimately, he said, he did check and correct some facts, and reordered a few points of chronology. He had read some reviews of *Bitter Fame*, and had gotten the impression that it was the first biography that portrayed Sylvia in all of her complexity, not just in a uniformly favorable light – it pointed out how self-defeating she could be, how difficult to live with..

"But she wasn't so difficult, not at all". He gazed down into the river water, with what looked like a fond, rueful smile. "Actually, she was quite cheerful, bright, even a bit – how too say this – diffident? She always went along with what others wanted. Only when jealous was she difficult – she'd fly into a rage, become almost someone else. But she was a very good mother, very devoted to the children". He pronounced "children" with an emphasis that conveyed the full gravamen of his fatherhood. Other companions and family members notwithstanding, he had been – I realized – the children's sole parent for most of their lives. And they, in turn, were his flesh-and-blood connection to Sylvia, their faces the mirrors out of which her face went on gazing into his.

Your son's eyes, which had unsettled us
With your Slavic Asiatic
Epicanthic fold, but would become
So perfectly your eyes,
Became wet jewels,
The hardest substance of the purest pain
As I fed him in his high white chair.
(from 'Life After Death')

Hughes continued to reminisce about their life together, and for an hour the sun seemed to stand still above the launch, above the river gliding away beneath it, above the entire turning world. There must have been a magic circle around us, because for that time no one on the crowded launch broke away from the throngs snacking and chattering elsewhere on deck to approach us. No one looking at us as we stood there could have discerned from our appearances – the tall, broad-shouldered man with silvering hair, dressed in a linen jacket, sports shirt and slacks; the small woman in an Indian *salwar kameez* of blockprinted cotton – that such an extraordinary conversation was taking place..

Hughes talked quietly, in measured tones, but all that he said was vivid, urgent – as if his subject were not a dead woman but a beloved friend and former lover who had recently moved to another city. He spoke of Plath with respect, admiration, affection – there were no traces of rancor or resentment. I was amazed: not only that he had so much to say, but that he would share his recollections with me, in a setting in which we were both sufficiently displaced from our usual circles even to meet and to have such a dialogue. Whatever I had previously read about this famous poetic couple, I wanted to divest myself of any prior notions and just listen. And what I heard were some of the stories surrounding the poems in process, the memories out of which, even as Hughes recounted them, the poems must have been growing.

"Yes, she was very easy to be with", Hughes said. "The thing about which she was most uncompromising – besides her poetry – was facing herself". She was completely fearless about confronting the devastating aspects of her own character, he said, no matter where her self-discoveries might lead.

In the myth of your first death our deity
Was yourself resurrected . . .
. . . Our newborn
was your own self in flames . . .
You were a child-bride
on a pyre.
Your flames fed on rage, on love . . .
And I was your husband
Performing the part of your father

In our new myth –

(from 'Suttee')

"She had tremendous physical courage as well", he said, and then chuckled as he recounted a curious incident from the days shortly before they met, in Cambridge in February 1956. Sylvia had been horseback riding a few times a week in the countryside around Cambridge, but since the stables were located down among the colleges, she had to ride through town to reach the country. On this occasion, her horse bolted and galloped back to the stable; Sylvia lost her stirrups, slipped out of the saddle, and started to fall, but somehow managed to hang on. "What a sight that must have been!" Hughes shook his head at the image of Sylvia clinging to the underside of the horse's neck

Carolyne Wright, A. U. M. Fakhruddin and Ted Hughes, November 1989

like a monkey as they galloped through the streets of Cambridge. Though the story was amusing, Plath could have been badly injured. But it had been quite the topic of conversation about town at the time, and Hughes was intrigued because he had just met her.

It was uncanny to hear this man in late middle age express his younger self's concern for the physical safety of a woman already decades dead.

. . . I can live
Your incredulity, your certainty
That this was it. You lost your

stirrups. He galloped
straight down the white line of the Barton Road.
You lost your reins, you lost your seat –
It was grab his neck and adore him
Or free-fall. You slewed under his neck,
An upside-down jockey with nothing
Between you and the cataract of macadam.
How did you hang on? You couldn't have done it.
Something in you not you did it for itself.

(from 'Sam')

"We were such *kids!*" Hughes exclaimed, shaking his head at the memory. They actually went to Westminster Abbey to get married, he said, because it was Sylvia's favorite place in all of London. They searched out the Dean – dragged him out of his study to perform the ceremony, with one friend as witness. The Dean took them aside and said, "Look here, this isn't how it's done". The young couple had no idea.

> . . . if we were going to be married
> It had better be Westminster Abbey. Why not?
> The Dean told us why not. That is how
> I learned that I had a Parish Church.
> Saint George of the Chimney Sweeps.
>   (from 'A Pink Wool Knitted Dress')

Hughes' voice was full of the amazement of those months of whirlwind courtship and marriage; for him, standing at that boat railing under the hot November sun of 1989, it was as if that amazement were still new, fresh:

>   You were transfigured.
> So slender and new and naked,
> A nodding spray of wet lilac.
> You shook, you sobbed with joy, you were
>   ocean depth
> Brimming with God . . .
> Levitated beside you, I stood subjected
> To a strange tense: the spellbound future.
>   (from 'A Pink Wool Knitted Dress')

What impressed me, listening to this story, was how these young people, barely in their mid-20s, had made such bold, definitive, adult decisions. "You'd never have been able to do such grown-up things", I thought aloud, "if you had believed you couldn't". Hughes nodded, and I realized that by November 1989, the number of years of the "spellbound future" that had passed since that transfigured Bloomsday 1956 wedding was a few more than the 30 years Plath had lived.

By now, the late-morning sun, shining directly down onto the deck where we stood, was beginning to burn; we moved into the shade. I was afraid that someone shouting out bids in the raucous "poem auction" in one corner of the cabin would notice us and approach. But no one paid any attention, so we negotiated a passage through the cabin without interference and continued our conversation at the deserted railing on the shaded side of the launch. It was in this shade, just beyond the poetic hubbub drifting from open portholes in the cabin, that Hughes' words took a profound turn.

"Yes, we did act decisively", he said, continuing the earlier thought. They had to, I thought – they didn't have much time: a little less than seven years from first meeting untill Plath's death. "The children were so young when she died", Hughes said, "one and three years old". They would now be 27 and 29 – the ages Plath was when she gave birth to them.

"It must have been very difficult for them", I said. Then, daring to empathize with her:

"And strange and difficult for her to leave them".

"Yes". Hughes' voice cracked a little with this affirmation. Her death had a great effect on them, he said, even though they were too young to understand what had happened. The boy had no memories of her at all.

> But his mouth betrayed you – it accepted
> The spoon in my disembodied hand
> That reached through from the life that had
>   survived you.
>
> Day by day his sister grew
> Paler with the wound
> She could not see or touch or feel, as I dressed it
> Each day with her blue Breton jacket.
>   (from 'Life after Death')

"Sylvia was a good mother, very devoted to the children", Hughes said again – a declaration that he repeated several times. In fact, much of his talk was of the children: their education, their adult lives, their bafflement over their mother's posthumous celebrity, their curiosity about what she was like as a person, and their incomprehension at having been, as it were, abandoned by the mother who, ironically, had always felt herself abandoned after her own father's death.

"Don't ever speak ill of your mother, I've told them", he said. "If not for her, you would never have been able to attend such good schools". Hughes went on to explain that, with the various books of hers, the royalties and the like, "we've gotten" – his voice deepened – "incredible sums". He hunched over the launch's railing and shook his head with wonderment.

"Ironic, isn't it", he went on, "because during her lifetime, she struggled to find a publisher". She sent her poetry collections again and again to

America, he said, and was rejected by editors there, until finally the British publisher Heinemann took a chance with *The Colossus*. At the time of her death, Plath was known only to a small circle of poets. All the fame, and income, came later, but at what cost. That was what many people had forgotten.

Hughes could very well have been talking about the conclusion of his poem 'Ouija':

"To please you and your mother", his younger self asks the Ouija-board spirit, "'Shall we be famous?'" Plath, horrified, snatches her hand back and rejects this question: "Don't you see – fame will ruin everything". The older Hughes, recalling this moment, wonders if her shock and dismay came because she was hearing, and recoiling from, a message from a source deeper than that of the Ouija spirit: the "still small voice" of her own intuition:

"Fame will come. Fame especially for you.
Fame cannot be avoided. And when it comes
You will have paid for it with your happiness,
Your husband, and your life."

(from 'Ouija')

Hughes has been harshly criticized, as executor of the Plath literary estate, for the pacing and quantity of materials he has edited and released for publication over the years. According to some, it has been too much; according to others, too little. But his comments on the deck of the *Rangapalli* were not the words of an heir-executor gloating over the profits, but of a man sorrowing over the uncountable cost that those "incredible sums" had exacted.

In the time she had, Hughes continued, Plath devoted herself to the children, but she became the mother they never knew. The girl, Frieda, remembered her for a few years, though.

Just as when your daughter, years ago now,
Drifting in, gazing up into my face,
Mystified,
Where I worked alone
In the silent house, asked, suddenly:
"Daddy, where's Mummy?" The freezing soil
Of the garden, as I clawed it.
All around me that midnight's
Giant clock of frost.

(from 'Visit')

In the heated breeze off the mid-day river – with its thick, alluvial smells of raw jute and threshed paddy, rotting fish and vegetable matter, bilge from passing barges, and curried chicken cooking for our lunch in huge pots in the *Rangapalli*'s galley – I shivered. The frosts and ice-slicks of that bitter English winter of 1963, the coldest in 60 years, seemed to be closing around us – where, after his wife's death, Hughes and his two orphaned children "made a deep silence / In our separate cots... We lay in your death, / In the fallen snow".

"You see, we had become. . . ." Hughes paused, and his voice modulated strangely. "We had become so close, we had worked together so closely, it was uncanny – as if we had become one person". He spoke with a tenderness still raw, his words hovering over the river like the echo of a lover's voice from a quarter-century past.

She wanted his assurance, weeping she begged
For assurance he had faith in her. Yes, yes. Tell me
We shall sit together this summer
Under the laburnum. Yes, he said, yes yes yes.

(from 'The Inscription')

They had told each other, he went on, that no matter what, even if there were physical separation, they could never really be apart, could never really be two separate people ever again. But then...

Over and over and over and over he gave
What she did not want or did
Want and could no longer accept or open
Helpless-handed as she hid from him
The wound she had given herself, striking at him
Had given herself, that had emptied
From her hands the strength to hold him against
The shock of her words from nowhere, that had
Fatally gone through her and hit him.

(from 'The Inscription')

I hardly dared to glance at him, but I did – and started slightly: in the spell his words had cast, I almost expected to see the gaunt, 32-year-old widower standing next to me, numb and haggard in the first access of grief. Instead, it was the middle-aged Hughes who leaned heavily on the railing, staring down into sunlight glinting off the glassy green wake unfurling from the *Rangapalli*'s prow. In profile, his face looked haunted; one lock of silvering hair fell forward over his brow.

"But then she was gone, and when I looked for her inside myself, where she'd always been, *she wasn't there*". He uttered these words in a tone of horrified wonderment. "There wasn't anyone there".

> Then I crept through the house. You never knew
> How I listened to our absence...
> The house made newly precious to me
> By your last lonely weeks there, and your crying...
> I listened, as I sealed it up from myself...
> I peered awhile, as through the keyhole,
> Into my darkened, hushed, safe casket
> From which (I did not know)
> I had already lost the treasure.
>
> (from 'Robbing Myself')

Hearing this, I was moved with as profound a sense of empathy and awe as any Shakespearean tragedy could have elicited. This was as close as anyone sharing such matters with me had ever come to conveying in words – quiet, understated, full of admiration and longing and regret nearly three decades vibrant – the tenor and texture of a life together. Hughes seemed to be a man chastened by the magnitude of what he had lost, under a life sentence of living in the long shadow of Plath's absence and, ironically, her continual life-in-death presence – not just in the recesses of his own memory, but in the incessant reminders breaking in from the outside world of media attention, critical acclaim, and detractors' opprobrium. I sorrowed for them both – "such kids!" he had exclaimed – who had loved each other so profoundly and who had both, in their own ways, abandoned or seemed to abandon the other – "broken the rules", as he called it.

"I've been writing out my own version of events", he went on, "but it will be published posthumously. If people knew the full story, when they learn what really happened between us, they'll be surprised that it's so mundane, so ordinary". After this, he lapsed into silence. We simply stood, gazing out over the river. Beyond the banks, the fields were flooded and green with half-grown shoots of the winter rice planting; or dry-soiled and giddy with mustard flower, the sudden brilliant sight of which is a Bengali idiom for being startled, for seeing stars. Then one of the Bangladeshi journalists approached us – hesitantly, almost on tiptoe, as if he could sense the reflective mood of the Poet Laureate and the woman standing next to him – to ask Mister *HUGE-es*, sir, if he could take a few snaps and ask a few short questions. Hughes turned to him with a patient smile, and the extraordinary conversation was over.

Unless Hughes was referring to another as-yet-unpublished writing, *Birthday Letters* is certainly not a document of any ordinary, mundane marriage. Even the closely observed minutiae of domestic life flash with the brilliance of 40-odd years of retrospection, and deepen with memory's double perspective, as the poet recreates his younger self trying to comprehend the inner significance of key gestures and words, and his older self wonders if anything could have happened differently. The voice in the poems is that of a man trying to plumb the depths of a beloved woman's gifted mind and troubled psyche: he still loves her, is still wounded by her, and profoundly shaken by her death. The tenderness in these poems is naked but expressed with the decorum of a long-familiar sorrow, as if grief and the poet have matured together, as if grief is the companion he has married in her stead.

It was clear to me then, in 1989, that Hughes would go on living with Plath in the only way now possible – in words, in memory – perhaps to the end of his days. In his reserved and understated manner, he was making a profound expression of the undying nature of love – of his love and respect and sorrow for the brilliant and tormented poet-wife of his youth. In his words to me, as in the poems he was even then writing, he was seeking a resolution to his own and their children's loss and grief, some way of coming to terms with his beloved's abrupt, irreversible departure from him, from her children, from herself. He seemed to seek no less than a reconciliation across the very boundary between life and death.

> It goes with me, your seer's vision-stone.
> Like a lucky stone, my unlucky stone.
> I turn it, a prism, this way and that.
> That way I see the filmy surf-wind flicker
> Of your ecstasies, your visions in the crystal.
> This way the irreparably-crushed lamp
> In my crypt of dream, totally dark,
> Under your gravestone.
>
> (from 'The Prism')

"What happens in the heart simply happens" – this insight comes to Hughes near the end of his poem 'Child's Park'. Bleak and serene at once, it seems to be the essence of tragic acceptance, and of the mature poet's enduring love, at the core of these heart-rending poems.

Totem Poll

IAN SANSOM ON THE MYTH OF TED HUGHES

The Epic Poise:
A Celebration of Ted Hughes

Edited by Nick Gammage
Faber and Faber, Pbk £9.99
ISBN 0 571 19686 1

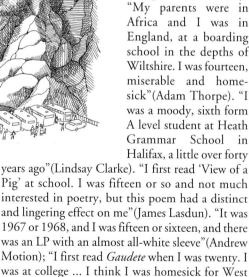

ATTEMPTING TO DESCRIBE the experience of reading a poem can be a bit like attempting to describe the taste of a peach, or God. What can you say but that a peach tastes peachy, which is merely to say that it does not taste like an apple or an orange, or that God is all that man is not, only more so? A peach, one might venture further, looks a bit like an orange, or an apple, and it has a skin and a stone and flesh, and the flesh is soft, and the stone is hard, and with rough handling the rot sets in.

The same might be said of a poem. Some people, for example, are content merely to describe what a poem reminds them of – usually other poems. Thus, Tom Paulin writing in *The Epic Poise*, unzips and squeezes Hughes's poem 'The Beach' until he extracts from it a few drops of Hopkins's 'The Windhover'. "What we find", claims Paulin, "is a kind of allusiveness that a has fresh-peeled, sappy, present-moment directness".

Others in *The Epic Poise* simply insist upon the exquisite rarity of the taste of Hughes's work. Thus, Melvyn Bragg's big wow about *Tales from Ovid*: "his great book", he enthuses, "the best present I have ever bought for myself". And yet others go into great detail discussing texture and structure:

"Throughout this poem there is a wonderful interplay of opposites: cold becomes heat, bone becomes iron, the inanimate becomes animate"(Raymond Briggs on 'Tractor').

Yet judging by the evidence of most of the contributions to *The Epic Poise* by far the most popular way of trying to describe a favourite thing, whether it be a poet, the personality, the Godhead, or a particular soft fruit, is to attempt to recall that point in time when the taste was first discovered, in the hope that the act of remembrance will help recover the meaning. For many of those contributing to the book this involves recalling an intensely private and usually miserable experience at private, public or grammar school, or at college or university. "My parents were in Africa and I was in England, at a boarding school in the depths of Wiltshire. I was fourteen, miserable and homesick"(Adam Thorpe). "I was a moody, sixth form A level student at Heath Grammar School in Halifax, a little over forty years ago"(Lindsay Clarke). "I first read 'View of a Pig' at school. I was fifteen or so and not much interested in poetry, but this poem had a distinct and lingering effect on me"(James Lasdun). "It was 1967 or 1968, and I was fifteen or sixteen, and there was an LP with an almost all-white sleeve"(Andrew Motion); "I first read *Gaudete* when I was twenty. I was at college ... I think I was homesick for West Yorkshire"(Simon Armitage).

This rather primitive, rather Protestant, and basically experiential approach to Hughes's work is not restricted merely to the great mope of students;

teachers get a look in too. "Very early on in my career as a primary school teacher, I read Ted Hughes's poem 'View of a Pig' to a class of eight and nine-year olds"(Wendy Cope). "Inevitably, I brought all of my teacherly preoccupations to my reading of *What is the Truth?*"(Jill Pirrie). "It was as a classroom teacher that I first read Ted Hughes's poetry, over thirty years ago"(Michael Morpurgo).

Even those few who didn't encounter Hughes's work in the classroom wish they had, or seem to feel they have to apologise for the fact that they didn't: "If I'd read Hughes at sixteen I might not have felt an aspiring writer had to move away from Yorkshire in order to work"(Blake Morrison); "If I were capable of being a teacher these are the poems I would bring into the classroom with me"(Susan Hill).

What does this tell us about the reading of poetry? Clearly, that a lot of it takes place in schools and perhaps, unless you're lucky, little after. This may be because poetry is something that only really happens to and impresses young people, much as opera and fine wines happen to and impress the middle-aged. Hughes himself, of course, was well aware of this. Christopher Reid, in his essay, unwittingly portrays Hughes as deliberately preying upon the young – "Young audiences, children, minds as yet undamaged by bad education, were what he seemed to prefer" – which is rather creepy.

Whatever his preferred taste in audiences, Hughes's poetry clearly continues to answer to some inner craving or desire which seems to have emerged for many his readers around about the time of adolescence. It may be that something gets broken in our minds in childhood, which poetry can help fix. Or perhaps we feel a lack of something at around the age of puberty which makes us prone to accept the kind of knowledge that Hughes's poetry proffers.

This thing, of course, is sex. The most honest responses to Hughes's work in *The Epic Poise* – responses which do more than merely add to the already existing stock of useless phrases about his work – spellbinding, mesmerising and electrifying – address this directly, registering and measuring the extraordinary erotic charge of the poems. Peter

> Christopher Reid, in his essay, unwittingly portrays Hughes as deliberately preying upon the young – "Young audiences, children, minds as yet undamaged by bad education, were what he seemed to prefer" – which is rather creepy.

Redgrove perhaps goes a little too far when he describes the famous thought fox as "a stealthy phallus"and the gnats in 'Gnat-Psalm' as "stating a continual orgasm of life", but nonetheless, even in the most chaste appreciations one can see stirring the sure signs of sexual arousal: Simon Armitage, for example, praises the penetration of *Gaudete*, claiming that "Hughes's words on the page travel right through the optic nerve, discharging something infinitely more profound".

For someone totally unread in Hughes – someone say, who didn't go to school in England during the 1960s or 1970s or 1980s – the impression that one would come away with from *The Epic Poise* would be the old one of Poet as Hero: macho, graceful, tender, violent, gentle, terrifying. Irene Worth describes Hughes as "mythic"; Lavinia Greenlaw calls him a "pole star"; A. Alvarez compares him to Heathcliff. The poetry is often compared to a force of nature, and is frequently associated with the rituals of birth and death. Writing about her experience of childbirth, for example, Medbh McGuckian, writes of *Moortown* that it was "one of the few texts ... that encompassed or came anywhere near confronting the harrowing and soul-splitting, body-shattering experience I had barely emerged from".

All such testimony is of course moving and impressive, but it is also misleading. No one – except Alvarez – admits that Hughes's great wisdom was closely related to folly and that he was prone to state things in verse that would have been totally unacceptable in prose. In a famous interview he once stated that "Any form of violence – any form of vehement activity – invokes the bigger energy, the elemental power circuit of the Universe". Any form of violence? – this is very troubling.

Hughes the hero may be dead, but the myth will undoubtedly persist. Laid low, he has already been erected as totem: Blake Morrison, for example, writes that it was "as if a giant oak had toppled, leaving only saplings below". It will be interesting to see what all the *Untermensch*, all us poor saplings, make of the oak once we're fully grown – assuming that our growth has not forever been stunted from standing too long in the shade.

The Geoffrey Dearmer Prize

SHEENAGH PUGH SELECTS THE *POETRY REVIEW*
YOUNG POET OF THE YEAR: SARAH WARDLE

COMPETENCE IS VERY well; one expects no less at this level, but I wanted to see language take off and fly. It doesn't very often; there are poets with distinguished careers whose words, for me, remain resolutely earthbound. You know flying when you see it, and it happens at many levels. I saw it in Deborah Randall's first collection *The Sin Eater*; in Alison Spritzler-Rose's poem 'Bukovina'; in a first-year student of mine whose flawed work is more fun than that of many published poets, because language does unexpected things in her hands.

I didn't find anything quite like the examples above among these seven. Yes, they were all competent and there were things I liked about each – Ros Barber's sparky language, Angela Leighton's control of rhythm, Cate Parish's metaphors, though I wish she wouldn't keep explaining what they're about in the last verse. But I was looking for reasons why six of them weren't going to win. Among these were (1) over-explanation, an urge to spell out what the poem's about instead of trusting the reader, (2) failure to transcend the anecdotal and personal and (3) a tendency to analyse the material to death so that one can't get a picture of the thing in question, only of the poet's mind reacting to it.

If I were like a Famous Poet with whom I've judged, I could have found another reason. She told me she would never consider a poem with a spelling error in it for a prize (I won't name her, but some folk might be surprised if I did). I thought this might be a bit harsh but now I'm not sure. I didn't expect, at this level, to see "aquduct" for "aqueduct", three times in one poem; "acquarium" for "aquarium" or "alot" for "a lot" (that might be a typo but I doubt it; my students do it all the time, along with "incase" and "atall"). It feels like a disrespect for words, a sense that they don't matter enough.

The winner, Sarah Wardle, stood out, for me, after the first two readings. Naturally I wasn't crazy for all 15 poems – there were a couple of nature-and-herby ones which seemed to be wearing kaftans and Seventies love-beads. But the control of form was impressive, as was the humour and lack of self-obsession; this poet looks out at the world rather than contemplating the inside of her head. More important still is the fact that the language lives, it's sparky and feisty; it always runs rather than plodding and now and then ('Young Man in Bronze'; 'Modern Poet') it flies.

The Geoffrey Dearmer Prize was instigated in 1997 in honour of the noted WWI poet and the Poetry Society's oldest member, Geoffrey Dearmer, who died in 1996. The first award was won by Paul Farley. Thanks to a generous bequest by Geoffrey Dearmer's family, the Prize will now be awarded annually. The Dearmer Prize Event, with Sarah Wardle and Sheenagh Pugh, will be at the Poetry Cafe, 6.30pm, November 17.

SARAH WARDLE

BORN IN LONDON in 1969, I spent much of my childhood on the edge of the industrial Midlands, went to school in Birmingham and Cheltenham and moved to Sussex. I read Classics at Oxford, where I was elected president of a political society. Then at twenty-one illness erupted in a series of acute episodes over four rollercoaster years. I recovered with the help of a very loving family. I have worked in various jobs: in an office, in a shop, as a teacher, on a farm, as a research assistant and in tourism. Reading and writing poetry became ever more important. I enrolled at Sussex University and two years later took a First in English, going on to an MA, and this year hope to begin a doctorate on Form and Tradition in Contemporary Poetry. I plan to combine teaching with writing.

TWO POEMS BY SARAH WARDLE
PSYCHE

Yesterday life was faster and fuller than this,
when I arrived here, barefoot, with clenched fist,
ready to kick and punch. Yes, I fought.
Having travelled the earth to find him, I was distraught,
seeking him who came to me divinely in the night,
always in darkness, invisible, so that it might
all have been a dream, but one I believed.

I journeyed here, hoping to be received
in this, his house, his palace, his temple,
with him at the top of the aisle by the oracle,
extending his hand like a bridegroom. It was a trick.
I tried to escape, ran down corridors, looked for an exit,
like Theseus without Ariadne's thread.

It was no good. I was surrounded,
trapped like an animal caught in the nets. I'd be fed
to the Minotaur, or to one of the heads
of the Hydra. By fighting I only made matters worse:
seven sentries appeared, where before was one nurse.

I climbed on the couches, knocked over a chair,
hid in an alcove to block out the glare
of a light. Cupid was nowhere. The voices of my sisters screamed,
"He's not your lover! He's a monster!" In a living dream
I'd become Odysseus in the Cyclops' cave,
about to be swallowed without a chance of being saved.

They said *No One* would hurt me, but I guessed their game:
I knew that *No One* was *Somebody*'s name.
They sharpened a needle for the eye of my mind,
speared it in, till I felt myself fade and go blind,
freefalling into a blackened abyss,
forever shut out from the day, like Oedipus.

Then I turned into Sisyphus pushing a rock,
as I struggled to keep awake, to swim back to the top.
Next I was Aeneas in Hades, the nurses were ghosts.
I was Psyche again when I awoke.

This room is silent now. On the door is a number
in washable ink. I wear a hospital toga.
When the nurse comes in with more drugs, she will say
in a mocking tone, "How is Aeneas today?"
Yes, yesterday with racing thoughts and clenched fist,
I can say life was faster and fuller than this.

IN THE NATIONAL PALACE MUSEUM, TAIWAN

Here in this entrepreneurial State
they work in night markets and evening school.
A Ming porcelain bowl shows Dragon Gate,
where a carp rises from a cobalt pool

to become that creature in mist above,
a symbol of strength, of the emperor,
of success – a concept these people love,
who fled from a communist conqueror.

In their port cargoes prepare to embark.
In their World Trade Centre the day's begun.
China Steel is the scale of a theme park.
Textile factory machines run and run.

But see how each busy capitalist
stares serenely through an exhibit's glass
to gaze at lotus flowers, a phoenix,
or philosophers on a mountain path.

ANGELA LEIGHTON

ANGELA LEIGHTON WAS born in Wakefield, brought up in Edinburgh and now lives in Hull where she teaches English at the university. The combination of a Yorkshire father and a Neapolitan mother left her with a legacy of conflicting languages and selves. She began writing poetry about ten years ago when her father died. Since then, in addition to various critical books, she has published poetry in *Poetry Review, London Magazine, The New Writer, Agenda, Borderlines,* among others. Both the theme and feel of foreignness are central to much of her work.

ANGELA LEIGHTON
ACCIDENT

Then, he ran into nowhere by mistake.
He took it by this sudden corner –
missed a larch, a gate, that wall,
just missed it all, though he had been,
all day, all life, on the track of it.

The road was in no hurry where it went
back or ahead, amending the rough hills
that happen, anyhow, backing up the sky's
easy outlets that clear everything:
road, remembering, one day going somewhere.

He stopped, just where the rest of us go on,
and scaled a second's gradient out of air –
a one-in√one no√one can take again. The lashed,
turned sadness of a larch, rain in its arms,
a gate, a wall, recall him, take him in.

SPILLS

These splintering yellows, greens – short straws
stooked in a clear glass – suddenly stop me
        dead, remembering:

fire, the catch of it *live* – the whet
and lick fetched to your pipe and embering
        breath rings.

A whipcrack, flick, and the sparks winked
starry-eyed just for a split-second tacked
       on the coal-black.

Spills made spells. We never guessed
their wish and flash might also slow-fuse
       quick to death.

A lump in my throat, seeing them there.
Spillikins, child's play. Yours, the pipe-dreams.
       Mine, cold spells.

ROS BARBER

BORN IN 1964, but brought up in Essex, Ros Barber works as a part-time
creative writing tutor for the University of Sussex. Her poetry has been
commended in both the Arvon and the National Poetry Competitions, and has
been anthologised by Faber (*Hard Lines 3*, 1987) and Virago (*Wild Cards: The
Second Virago Anthology of Writing Women*, 1999). Magazine credits include
Poetry Review, London Magazine, MsLexia and *Orbis*. She has had short stories
published in anthology form by Bloomsbury and Serpent's Tail, and won second
prize in this year's Asham Award for short fiction by women. She was a prize
winner in the 1997 *Independent on Sunday* short story competition.

TWO POEMS BY ROS BARBER
EVE'S HOBBY

Love's circumstantial scraps
blooming like funeral lilies on
my sheets began it: the avarice.

When I couldn't bear to wash free
his parting shot; when I couldn't
bring myself to purity, I fell to this.

Others collect mail-order figurines,
porcelain bears or reproduction
coins: untender things. But I

catalogue what others have
and I have not. The scent of sex
drifting across suburban gardens,

tangled in stunted fruit trees.
The elsewhere smile of the girl
waiting for a bus in flesh tone tights.

The couples half-having it through
clothes on the slopes of the park:
tendril limbs, tongues buried deep

in each other's mouths. And then there's
the matter of fact. Banana-coloured condoms
by the bandstand:

I pick them up when no-one's looking.
Latex stretched to the shape of desire
moulded to the cocks of strangers;

those prized, thickening globes of semen,
and the crusting juices
of women men entered but did not fill.

Summer finds me sprawled, awake,
across his ancient imprint, windows
gaping for new and precious

additions: the lilt of bedsprings
in the pilot's upstairs apartment,
the bruising chill of unexpected laughter.

NEW BOY

He is walking a line; his footsteps mark a square
around the playground. The others forget his name:
a boy that isn't really anywhere.

Wherever he was just then, he isn't there
but somewhere further along, just out of frame.
He is walking a line; his footsteps mark a square

enclosing his teacher, enclosing the autumn air.
She blames no-one, knowing she cannot blame
a boy that isn't really anywhere.

He is more than alone. While other children pair
off by the fence and a penalty kicker takes aim,
he is walking a line. His footsteps mark a square

like the edge of a board, a game of solitaire.
He doesn't seem to know another game.
A boy that isn't really anywhere

is on the perimeter. You'd think he doesn't care
about being different. But still, and just the same,
he is walking a line; his footsteps mark a square,
a boy, that isn't really anywhere.

HUGH MACPHERSON

HUGH MACPHERSON WAS born in Edinburgh in 1953. He received a Scottish
Arts Council Writer's Bursary in 1988 and the National Library of Scotland's
Robert Louis Stevenson Award in 1998. His poems, stories and articles have
been published in some thirty magazines and papers – including *Stand*, *The
Rialto*, *Poetry London*, *Poetry Review*, *The Scotsman* and the *Times Literary
Supplement* – and broadcast on Radio 4. A former diplomat, he has translated
from Swedish, Turkish, Portuguese, Latvian, Croatian and French, and written
about a wide range of countries across Europe and the Middle East.

TWO POEMS BY HUGH MACPHERSON
THE WEATHER IN EUROPE

In the heart of town flags flap
outside parliament and government,
where piles of paper poise under
twenty four hour neon to promulgate
and proclaim. I watch the police guards
huddle in their booth to avoid the rain
as I dodge last dregs of ice that still
slide off the rooftops. Poles across
the sidewalk warn that even parliament
can't rule where frozen snow chooses
to fall, while riddles of ice water thrum
along the rones, wriggle through metal pipes

with the tuck and rhythm of a jazz drum
before they escape across paving stones
in sparkling runnels that illuminate the day.

An hour up the road from here
they speak another language, will turn
our car into a brief border incident
as they consider what foreign devilments
we bring. But on the weather map
there's no difference, and in their old town
meltwaters round the castle swirl with
identical sound as they too tame frozen winter,
while flags heavy with this same soothing rain
lap the evening air in glad gestures of experience,
their boastful, booming breathing celebratory
above the cries of circling children
and the slow footsteps of evening couples out
to take the measure of this weather system
that liltingly unfreezes the heart of Europe.

THE WOODEN MANOR

Now we're far from the Baltic,
but the country has taken on
some of that closed mystery
of the sea which brings you to a north
where light stays all summer,
while perspectives change and shimmer
behind the perpetual ridges where
the trees hold strange communication
as leaves share augury.

The wooden manor has paintings
on its walls of what was seen here
when the clock first started marking
time in 1653, and the figures stare out
still as though noting sharply the changes
that they've endured. There's the tall tower
of the Chinese tea pavilion – the fashion
that reached them in eighteen something
and stands proud above the oak trees

to remind the whole countryside
of how conversation was conducted
in the wider world, as it sipped
its latest brew. The corridor holds
photos of the revolution and the school
that fitted snugly in the manor house
until that administration too received
its marching orders, and the building
discreetly took a step back to the woods.

The planks themselves show tendencies
to join the forest floor again:
the wind-whispers that run around
skirting boards and the gaping stairs
already mimic the sounds of the world
outside. Those conversations between trees
which this part of the earth rejoices in
are taking hold once more. The heron
lifts up from the still lake and becomes sky.

V. G. LEE

I WAS BORN in 1949, and started writing about nine years ago. I've had poems published in several anthologies and magazines, including *Beyond Bedlam, The Exeter Poetry Prize Anthology, Poetry London,* and *Magma Poetry Magazine.* In 1998 I was a finalist for the Housman Poetry Competion. I also teach Creative Writing at Centerprise in Hackney.

TWO POEMS BY V. G. LEE

EMPTY SPACES
to Edward Hopper

His name is "Bill Old Thing" which presupposes
a roomy jacket on a kindly, generous natured chap.
Probably a sense of humour – ripe and full bodied –
can take the joke, can pass it back with interest.

It must be evening. Even quite late at night.
The bright, false light from the street
has shot a window image on the wall;
four flat, almost yellow rectangles
cauterised by a charcoal greyish cross.

Unnoticed, a door has opened into the room;
another rectangle, this time black.
A tall woman holds the door half open,
her fist on the brass handle
like a knot at the end of a piece of string.

Tonight she wears a purple and mustard
combination of foulard blouse
with pleated skirt. In the flapper era
she was the only one, among several
friends to insist on ankle-length dresses.

She still has a horror of bare flesh, nor does she
care much for the smile on Bill Old Thing's face,
which doesn't bother him in the slightest.
He retains his joie de vivre and rightly so:
experience tells him he can't be bettered.

Waiting in the doorway, she doggedly
maintains her position. This is not life.
This doesn't happen every day. At this particular
moment, it is happening. She steps backwards.
Pulls the door shut in her own face.

The door disappears.
"Cheerioski", Bill says.
He moves towards the window.
He is thinking of her.
Now he is not thinking of her.

SMILE

When at long last the daystar burns blue
and the sun splits the ice – I'm ready
to splash hot kisses on the face
of every man, woman, Jack in the bus,

bamboozle their sleepy senses
with lewd lyrics set to a tune
that everyone knew, but until that
very second thought happily forgotten.
To love with violence and with patronage,
spew laughter, refreshing as warm spindrift,
over god's winter-worn out,
desperate-for-fags, woolly-hatted,
half-hibernating creatures.
I sit hard down on my excitement –
wipe a way through the smeared window.
Mankind snores or attends to its ears
as two collarless dogs embrace.
I smile. My first smile of the year –
the size and shine of a partial eclipse.
On a morning like this, when at long last

R. G. BINNS

R. G. BINNS was born in Harrogate, Yorkshire, in 1948; was educated at Portsmouth Polytechnic and the University of East Anglia; has lived and worked in Canada and Nigeria; and since 1979 has lived in London. A first collection, *Time Upon a Once*, was published in 1998 by Zoilus Press.

TWO POEMS BY R. G. BINNS
A MAZE

Were you Alice, were you, then, that day, that final day?
In that flat where you liked the curtains drawn, where,
On that final day, the green blind was down in the kitchen,
The curtains drawn in your bedroom at two and at four
In the afternoon, and the rain coming down with a hiss
Like the hiss that came over the speakers when it ended,
The long-playing record, going click, click, click like
The seconds, like a metallic pulse, the player's heart.

Twenty winters later someone is dying who is old.
Arterial blood in the kidneys. Won't last beyond the weekend.

Doesn't. This is what you missed. The slowness of the years &
The slowing down. Marriage, children. Holidays abroad.
The deaths of family and friends. You were the first.
You'd be surprised that nowadays an LP seems
As obsolete and strange as a brittle 78. But some of the songs
You loved go on, go on. And I, so far, survive; remembering.

The player was a Bush, with a silver grille like a Ford's
& from it came Cat Stevens, Cohen, the Incredible String Band.
You listened in the dark. You told me you preferred autumn
And winter to spring or summer, you liked long coats & boots
Of black leather, snow, days of rain, days like that October
When the streets were washed with a crackling surf of orange
& yellows, and those trees in the long street were black & bare
As that empty beach where, at intervals, a far light flashed.

At forty-eight: orts. Numbers of all kinds pressing down
Upon those days. Mortality-scoured, you might say, this maze,
Considering the sunlight on a pale green sheet, a willow,
That spotted, paint-splashed fallen leaf, a sparrow on the grass.
I recall a bench at six a.m., jewelled with droplets; the milkman
Coming along in his float, selling us a cool pint. The first
Warm bread from that baker's when it opened.
A far light flashed. It's cold, so cold. I walk and walk

That beach where bubbles broke at our feet, where your boots
Got wet, where chains of unlit bulbs rattled on the esplanade,
Which was empty, where the plastic palm trees swayed
In the gusts, freezing, which followed us along that coast road
And inland, back to that city. On that final day it was cold, too,
And raining, the postman hurrying by, the wipers going
Backwards and forwards on all the cars, a slip-slop sound,
A hissing. A hissing. And a strange smell leaking into the hall.

I do not remember the trees at all. I was surprised to find them
There, blocking a view of the house. How they'd grown,
Year after year. I had no memory of the lock-up garages either.
I regretted going. The house still looked the same
But I didn't want to see inside. Besides, I had a train to catch.
The nineties aren't the seventies. So much has changed, Alice.
You never do. Those tiger's eyes, that warmth. That coat
The moths can't touch. A pipe that drips and needs a plumber.

The kitchen reminded me of an aquarium, that green murk
And the wet floor from a leak under the sink. The gas cooker
Was greasy and old; the landlord only called for the rent.
Year after year no one cared about the tears, the stains,
The chipped bowls. That sludge accumulated in the open drain.
Year after year the students came and went. That year
It was you. You never left. You're there still. Young
As you were, as you'll always be. But it was no place to die.

Your mother said she didn't like it from the start. That first day
She drove you there, with your suitcase and trunk and books.
Things seemed to go okay that first year, though. You made
Friends. You read classic Russian novels and bought LPs.
You kept the curtains closed. There's a lot I'm not saying,
Not yet; a lot I'm keeping out of this. Let's just say today
I'm listening in the dark, on an obsolete machine, hearing again
That hiss, that click, and chains of unlit rattling bulbs.

The curtains drawn at four; at six. Unopened until the doctor
And the police arrived. It made page two in the local paper,
And – Enough. . . The lights go on. My wife is home. I kiss her,
Help her with her coat. In the kitchen, I play a Nick Cave CD,
Prepare the evening meal. Later I'll check out a website,
E-mail a friend, tape that soap for my daughter. Drive to
Collect my son and forget again, again, if you were Alice, then,
That cold rain-drenched day when the green blind was down.

KITSILANO TRANSFER

Kitsilano Transfer? A wailing begins
Along the thistled tracks. She sucked his
Pencil. Ecks begins to see her name
Everywhere. From the winter's core

He grips his ballpoint and begins. Gives up.
Sits in the dark and watches an old movie,
Her cold hand in his hot hand. An old owl starts
To hoot incessantly. And moans. Time, time.

Bellowing at the windy distances a big
Bronchial wrinkled beast lies down to die.
Who is that who dances on a river of fire?
One who hasn't aged. One who once waited

At a crossroads for a train which didn't stop.
At the end of that rusting line is an overgrown dock
And a night journey across a sea where
Bearded mines bob, and it gets colder

And colder, and sluggard bergs ache, split,
And a father sleeps in a grey afternoon.
A war burns inside him. Khaki, blackened tanks,
Coupons. Stained plinths tattooed with

Dead numbers and names. Dreary insincere angels
Imprisoned in concrete, crosses beginning to tilt.
An old man boils potatoes in a pan.
There are no conclusions, only ruins.

CATE PARISH

I'M A TRANSPLANTED American. Somehow I find myself changed into a patio plant in southeast England. Plants and animals and the human relation to those interests me more than nationality. I lead a pretty ordinary life. I'm too busy, but I like nothing better than having nothing to do. I write to try to get beyond the mundane particulars of my life. I think that our times are giving rise to some exciting poetry; contemporary poets I like include Hans Magnus Enzensberger, Wisława Szymborska, Kenneth Koch and Frank Kuppner. I'm not claiming influences. I've had a number of individual poems published and a pamphlet from Flarestack last year; this year I won first prize in the Keats/Shelley Memorial Society's poetry competition.

TWO POEMS BY CATE PARISH
RIPE WAS THE DROWSY HOUR

It's not just that other people call upon one's services
when one is most loathe to provide them;
it's that even the ground beneath one' s feet is calling out
to be dug, or drained, or relaid with paving slabs;
there's no garden but that which extracts
the sweat of one' s brow to water itself.
In fact the entire universe will slump
without one's own best efforts to prop it up.
Even the most securely-tied shoelaces
work themselves loose and must be re-tied

in a complicated little manoeuvre it took years to master;
this in the midst of all the other little manoeuvres
that require the choreography of so many muscle-groups
it leaves one prostrated with exhaustion
just to think about it. Where are the heralded robots?
Why is the enthusiastic, hard-working person still urgently required?
To whip paper out of the photocopier, to brisk
across the room on clicky heels; smiling, god, smiling fit to bust,
snapping along like some kind of yacht in a stiff breeze,
when really one ought to be paid to breathe.

SOME LOSE THEIR HEARTS

When I saw the starfish
alone on the shore, I honed right in.
There was only one of it, and one of me,
as far as the eye could see. My eye.
The starfish didn't identify
with my eye, it was my hand it fell

instantly in love with. I was giving it a hand
back into the sea. Probably it was expecting
a bill or a snout, not something so like
itself. What was for me only a handshake
was for it a whole-body experience:
from the hundreds of tubefeet that rapturously
gripped me, a super-glue-like substance began to leak . . .

Intemperate passions make appalling messes
that need somebody to clean them up.
People ask me, why don't you do something.
Appalling messes everywhere you look,
and you, just walking along,
with your hands in your pockets.
There is nothing in my pockets, I tell them,
nothing at all.

A Different Drummer

ATTILA DÖSA INTERVIEWS DOUGLAS DUNN

Don't weary me
With "reputation", "text", "context", or "fame";
Don't "-ize", or "-ism" me; don't "theory" me...
('Disenchantments')

"An uneasy dialectic ... pervades Dunn's poetry, with a lyrical self in tension with public utterance", writes Colin Nicholson. It is true that in his criticism Douglas Dunn distinguishes the kind of poetry which depends more on personal lyrical impulses from that which is engaged with more particularly social issues. It is also true that he believes an overwhelming social interest on the part of the poet is likely to have potentially restrictive effects on poetry; for example, an awareness of reading the work of a politically committed poet may considerably reduce the reader's horizon of expectations. What may be even more harmful, however, is that the poet's awareness of particular social, political or critical expectations can affect the way he or she would naturally respond to inner artistic incentives, thus coercing a sense of living up to those expectations. Though representations of various social, political issues abound in Douglas Dunn's poetry, he refuses to submit himself to principles other than that which arise from inner aesthetic and moral convictions. He is more willing to assume even the role of the outsider (as evident in the personae of the *Terry Street* poems) than being programmatic in any way. In this sense, we may accept that there exists a dialectic of public and private references of art in his own poetry. But using the adjective "uneasy" when speaking about Douglas Dunn's poetry and convictions can hardly be seen as other than unbecoming. He is one of the most "relaxed" and independent minded poets of his generation; the only extraliterary expectation to which he is willing to conform is the expectation of a high moral standard. I asked Douglas Dunn about certain public as well as some more literary issues which, in one way or another, can be seen as relevant to understanding his poetry.

Attila Dösa: You are a critic of strong convictions, and can be seen as one of those few poet-critics who are consistent enough to distinguish the self who writes poetry from the self who approaches it. At the same time you are rather reticent about your own poetry. Your much appraised anthology of twentieth-century Scottish poetry has been reviewed flatteringly to have one weakness only: that you did not include some of your own poems in it. Why does that representative collection of Scottish verse not contain some of the acclaimed poems of the anthologiser?

Douglas Dunn: Modesty is not necessarily a virtue, but I wouldn't want to claim it as my vice either. I just happen to believe that if you edit an anthology, then the editor should have the decency to absent his poems from the selection. I mean, how can you "discuss yourself"? A good anthology is an act of criticism, and to have included my own poems would have been unreasonable and unwise. When I made my decision, I thought of Samuel Goldwyn's deathless remark, "Include me out", and thought, too, that it means much the same if you say (or if I say) "Exclude me in". I offer you William Plomer's epigram, 'Positive', which shows you the sort of thing I've observed in rather too many contemporary poets, and which I'm dedicated to avoiding ever being said of me.

His self-esteem has outrun calculation:
you'd make the biggest fortune ever known
if you could buy him at your valuation –
and sell him at his own.

AD: Your poetry is widely read abroad. Your poems have been translated into French, Italian, Hungarian, Polish, German, Czech, Bulgarian, and other languages. How do you feel about being translated?

DD: It's heartening, and a real compliment, to find my poems translated into other languages. Or that's what I feel. Sometimes translation coincides with a visit to another country and an opportunity to meet poets and readers there. Although I've become a bad traveller the older I get, I love it once I've arrived and acclimatized. That poetry should have an international audience is encouraging.

AD: What are the implications of your poems being read by audiences with different sociocultural backgrounds?

DD: Feeling and intelligence associated with love, death, places, and so on, tend to be much the same everywhere. Even if different cultural traditions condition them differently, it has to be said that such feelings are human more than national.

AD: In general, to what extent do you believe a European appreciation is important to a Scottish poet?

DD: My poems are also read in Australia and the United States, and I've recently returned from a literary visit to Venezuela. Perhaps I should widen your question beyond Europe. But I feel myself to be European, and I feel myself committed to an idea of Europe that is cultural before it is economic or political. To know that some of my poems have been read by those familiar, in mother tongues, with the works of Goethe, Heine, Rilke, Ronsard, Racine, Hugo, Baudelaire, &c., József, Pushkin, Pasternak, Mickiewicz, Lorca, Leopardi, Montale, and so on, is truly exhilarating.

AD: You have translated poetry into English, too, from French, and you have also translated some poems from Polish. You wrote among others a long poem in celebration of European culture, and broader cultural references are an invariable presence in your criticism as well as your poetry. How do you perceive the role of the poet as a mediator between cultures?

DD: My expertise in languages other than English is limited, and I couldn't claim a role as a mediator between cultures. About the best I can hope for is to represent my own culture as I understand it and try to do so honestly. But part of my mind and temperament – more so, I feel, than my "inheritance" as a Scot – is an interest in any poetry no matter where it comes from.

AD: What is the cultural significance of poetic dialogues between various languages?

DD: When I've attended poetry festivals or other events abroad I usually come away from them with a sense, not so much of difference, but of shared values and shared concerns. Poetic procedures and emphases of style may differ, but it is what is held in common that impresses me.

AD: Which poets and prose writers do you regard as your literary models?

DD: As for "models", I've tried to be my own man. If you mean "influences" then there are so many that I wouldn't know where to begin. Is it possible to suggest Shakespeare as an "influence" or "model" and not be laughed at? I find myself to be eclectic. Of the writing of this century I agree with Brodsky that W. H. Auden was probably the great genius in the English language. It was my privilege to know Philip Larkin on terms of friendship, but I wouldn't claim him entirely as a "model". Writers like Jonson, Marvell, Dryden, Pope, Burns, Scott, Wordsworth, Byron, Keats, Browning, Thomas Hardy, Robert Frost, Edwin Arlington Robinson, Robert Lowell, D. J. Enright, Ted Hughes, Peter Porter, and many others, have also been important to me, as have the earlier Scottish writers of the late mediaeval and Renaissance periods, and Scottish poets of the eighteenth century, plus Sir Walter Scott and Robert Louis Stevenson. It's against that more indigenous reservoir of "influences" and "models", that I've introduced writing from other cultures. I see "influence" as a turbulent and unsettled phenomenon.

AD: In the Greek poet C. P. Cavafy's poem 'Waiting for the Barbarians' we can read that the longed for coming of the barbarians, who represent a refreshing impact on a decadent society, could have been "a kind of solution". Do you perceive the existence of a broader European cultural context for the "barbarian" poetry written in the British Isles?

DD: I think I coined the term "barbarians" in a poetic context in the mid-1970s when I wrote the first part of my collection *Barbarians* (1979). Tony Harrison was in the same district of thought and feeling at the time, and Seamus Heaney also (perhaps even a little earlier). I used the term to mean the oppositional or socially and politically hostile aspect of contemporary poetic sensibility, which was shared chiefly by poets of a working-class and/or non-English origin in the British Isles. A friend of mine calls this the "hairy-arsed school of poetry", although how he knows is a bit of a mystery to me. In much of Central and Eastern Europe, the same "opposition" was expressed, but by far less direct means, by "Aesopian" or semi-secret routes. In the North-West European Archipelago poetry was capable of a greater directness although it could be instructive to notice its protective ironies as well.

AD: In particular, can we read Cavafy's poem as a subtext of the work of those poets who employ linguistic, ideological, political strategies subversive of Anglocentric value relations, or is that poem relevant to the present relationship between Scottish and English writing in any sense?

DD: Cavafy's poem wasn't foregrounded in my mind. My notion of "barbarians" came straight from the Greek, through bar-bar, the uncouth sounds of the languages of those who weren't Greek and were, allegedly, uncultured. The relationship between English and Scottish literature wasn't a priority. At the time, I was living in Hull, in East Yorkshire, and although the poems are aware of my Scottish background and concerns, I was more conscious of the offence of class-based politics and systems organized around the apparent psychological need for demeaning and humiliation on the grounds of birth, nationality, and accent.

AD: To look at it from a different angle, is it necessary to define who the "barbarians" are? Is it not the dynamic of the relationship that can be artistically more important and productive?

DD: "Barbarians", in the poems I wrote around that title and concept, are those who have otherwise been exluded from High Culture, but who, by the later part of the twentieth century in the North-West European Archipelago, come to possess it, very much to the embarrassment of those who assume that they have inherited and own the language and its poetic possibilities. Indeed, what you call "the dynamic" of the rela-

tionship' is where anything artistic might happen – or may have done, as this is an aspect of my work which is now in the past. At the same time it is part of my mind that could be re-activated if circumstances required it or mind and imagination conspired to bring it back to me. You seem to indicate a tension between "High" Culture and the concerns of "the people", and I would agree. I want to be a poet of High Culture but at the same time I don't want to be disloyal to my native parish, my home, my most immediate people, children, friends.

AD: In her *Britons: Forging the Nation 1707-1837*, Linda Colley's explanation for the contemporary re-emergence of diverse nationalist movements in the British Isles as opposed to the loss of an inclusive, British national identity – that, basically, as a member of the European Community Britain as a whole is no longer able to define itself against the states of Continental Europe – seems to be logical. Is "Britishness" an appropriate paradigm in reading contemporary Scottish writing, or has it ever been one?

DD: "Britishness" is a concept that has perplexed me in my adult years. It didn't bother me at all when I was younger. For example, when I was a schoolboy, I was in something called The Sea Cadet Corps. Many weekends were spent at a naval anchorage on the Firth of Clyde, while each summer we spent a fortnight on a ship of the Royal Navy. In my case it was HMS Diana, a 'D' class destroyer, based at Loch Foyle at Londonderry in Northern Ireland, from where we sailed to Gibraltar and back with units of the Home Fleet, and HMS Starling, a very famous frigate of the Second World War, flagship of Admiral Vian, a great scourge of German U Boats in its time, but by then a navigational training ship, and in which I sailed from Portsmouth to Randers in Denmark and then back to Harwich. I remember feeling very Royal Navy and very British. That I also felt very Scots didn't come into the equation even if companions called you "Porridge" or "Jock" or commented on your accent. You simply spoke back and held your end up. It strikes me that I've been doing the same ever since. I have to consider your question as pragmatically and as experienced as that. Poetry doesn't arise from a theory but from what the poet knows in life more than in intellect. Yet I have to admit that a "British" national identity may well be in question but due – and this is empirical rather than "historical" in a broad sense as conveyed by Linda Colley's book – to the puzzlement of English people at the rise of a post-imperial multi-racial society, the erosion inflicted by the Provisional I.R.A., Ulster Loyalists, and other terrorist factions in Ireland with their adjunct activities on the mainland, the so-called National Party in England with its fascist and Nazi affiliations, and far less to the convictions of the Scottish National Party. Scottish Nationalism is distinguished in Europe for its democratic principles and procedures. It hasn't killed anyone while no one as far as I know has died for its cause in this century unless through stress, overwork, or disappointment. What I'm saying is that the nationalism with which I'm familiar is benign, and not to be confused with nationalisms elsewhere or their lethal activities.

It's not so much a question of "Britishness" or "Britishism" as of the English language. Scotland admits to three languages – English, Scots and Gaelic. The first of these is a *lingua franca*, but with a Scottish accent (although sometimes with an English accent), and it is the language in which I write and speak (with a Scottish accent), although I have a facility to speak in Scots if I feel like it or the social context invites me to do so. I've never been embarrassed by this fact, which I acknowledge, simply, as a fact. But "Britishness" fails to offer a paradigm to a reading of contemporary Scottish writing. Why? – I believe the reason to be a matter of class politics among Scotland's writers and readers as much as nationalism.

AD: To carry it further, in the mind of a Scottish poet does European unification coincide with the loss of a (presumed or real) British national identity, and does he perceive it as a "loss" at all?

DD: I don't believe it's necessary for any national identity to undergo significant erosion as a result of the tendency towards European unity. Nor, for example, do I intend to change publishers or lose my friendships in England. Just how much difference there will be between today's status quo and a post-devolution state of affairs remains to be seen.

AD: A considerable portion of recent Scottish critical (as well as creative) writing is dedicated to the re-definition of the meaning of Scotland as a political, cultural, historical entity. What is your opinion about this intense – politically and socially not disinterested – debate about Scottishness?

DD: A debate about Scottishness has been going on for a very long time – ever since the run-up to the Treaty of Union of 1707. I'd just as soon stop talking and do something, but then I feel I don't want to try to be in any way politically "influential". There's something in me that resists "simplifying myself" (as Turgenev put it) in order to be a political activist. It's a debate in which I've played little part other than through whatever's represented in my writing. Were I to stand on public platforms and say in prose some of the things I've said in verse, then not only would I be paraphrasing my verses, and repeating myself, but I'd be surrendering to a topical force inferior to the art I represent and to which I've dedicated my life. I don't know why – it could be reckless, or feckless – but I feel brave enough to say that.

AD: "Scotland is a political fiction", you wrote in 1988. "It has its varieties of place, people, temperaments, languages, its cities, landscapes, its business, its industry, its employed and unemployed, its rich and poor – it has everything except citizenship." Would political independence be helpful in bringing Scotland's perplexing view of itself to a solution?

DD: Renan (I think) defined a nation as "a large-scale solidarity". Clearly, a country needs a nationality and citizenship to stand behind. Also, a country has to be in a position to take

> To try to write poetry at the present time obliges a poet to confront and struggle with a range of technical, formal issues, interwoven through the poet's thematic, emotional and intellectual obsessions. In the act of writing, the substance which a poet tries to shape – like wayward clay on a potter's wheel, handled by an apprentice potter – is both what the poet is trying to say and the technical means by which the poet tries to form the poem.

responsibility for itself; it shouldn't have to endure secondary status. Part of Scotland's trouble has been the willingness of so many of its people, in all walks of life, to behave as if second rate or inferior. I don't feel second rate, and I don't feel inferior. Boasting is not my style, and that's not my game here. Moaning and whingeing are conditions which I loathe and detest. I take full responsibility for my life and its decisions. Scotland is a country and a nationality into which I feel proud to have been born.

AD: How do you imagine the cultural role of an independent Scotland in Europe?

DD: Scotland's cultural role in Europe would, I hope, continue as at present and much as it always has. For a country of its size, its influence on Europe, and the world, has been big.

AD: We can read more and more about the definition as well as justification of the identities of various regions within Scotland. We could already get used to the way that Scottish writers are identified in literary criticism: through the identification of the regions or cities or islands they come from. The language of a Scottish writer – apart from social varieties and his or her choice of the three indigenous languages of Scotland – is basically described in terms of the regional variety deployed in his or her writing. Some even question if there is such a thing as "Scottishness".

AD: In the currently fashionable critical discussions of "Scottish identity" is not there a danger of these regional concerns' leading to a deconstruction of national concerns?

DD: Regional identities within Scotland may be overstated by those who identify with these regions, to the detriment of a truly national picture. From the perspective of literature, however, it's a commonplace view that you have to be local before you can succeed in being universal. Writing that's local and stays local will probably be of interest only to readers in that locality. Personally, I feel that to be a serious problem only if an attempt is made to claim universality for works that clearly don't possess it.

AD: As a poet who began his career in Hull and now is living in Tayport, Fife – always as far from metropolitan centres as possible, you've been sensitive to claims of provincialism and nationalism. Throughout his criticism Robert Crawford is very keen on making the concept of

"provincial" into a "term of praise". But, because of its negative undertone, Crawford abandons it for another term, "identifying poets", in his book of the same title. Thus he establishes a new paradigm for interpreting regional poets, deliberately devolving authority from the centre to what had previously been seen as periphery. He ranks you with Norman MacCaig, Sorley MacLean, and Seamus Heaney, whom he regards as "identifying poets" in the sense that they represent the identities of certain regions in their writing. However, is it not a restrictive reading, which foregrounds certain strains of territorial and social concerns to the detriment of other, aesthetic ones?

DD: I now live in Dairsie, smaller even than Tayport, and distant from metropolitan centres. It's a temperamental thing with me – I don't like living in cities, although I enjoy opportunities to visit them from time to time. Much of my writing refers to places and people, which comes naturally to me. Perhaps it's simply part of the apparatus I need in order to express my formal and aesthetic concerns. To try to write poetry at the present time obliges a poet to confront and struggle with a range of technical, formal issues, interwoven through the poet's thematic, emotional and intellectual obsessions. In the act of writing, the substance which a poet tries to shape – like wayward clay on a potter's wheel, handled by an apprentice potter – is both what the poet is trying to say and the technical means by which the poet tries to form the poem. It's hard to take one's mind off either of them, so that criticism which neglects a poet's artistry for the sake of chasing after an idea (no matter how interesting the idea) always seems to me to be incomplete. Or it could just be that a readable, technical criticism is difficult to achieve.

AD: Even in what seem to be your most regionally dedicated poems there is an ambition to attribute universal significance to the local and the particular. Can we say that the way to the comprehension of the individual leads through the comprehension of the universal in your poetry?

DD: I work in a University that was founded in 1411/12, and which is recognized as one of the major Universities of Europe and perhaps of the world. It's a very well known University – so I don't feel conscious of being on the periphery except perhaps in an imaginative sense. But I discover within myself the same germ of freedom, style, of self-challenge, that I find myself impressed by in a writer like Robert Louis Stevenson. Did Sir Walter Scott feel peripheral? Did Stevenson? Did Robert Burns for that matter? – I suspect Burns's localism to have been a tactic calculated by a powerful intellect simply to make it known that he existed. But I'm glad you see a wider frame of reference in my work. Throughout my writing life I feel I've engaged as much as has been possible for me with European literatures. I've always had to work hard for my living and so I've never enjoyed the leisure or the means to cultivate some of my interests as much as I would have liked. It annoys me, but my Samoa will always be one of the mind. Besides, in mid-life, I've discovered that I'm a practical man as much as a poet. Or practical-poetic. Or poetic-practical.

AD: Allegations of provincialism rarely take into consideration that geographical periphery is not necessarily the same as cultural periphery. But can a contemporary Scottish poet afford nowadays to disregard debates about provincialism and regionalism? Are you irritated by the subject?

DD: If I don't disregard them some of the time then I don't see how I can get anything written, because far from everything I write is addressed to "the matter of Scotland". But I'm not irritated by the presence of these arguments. Any writer lives and works in a specific intellectual and political climate and it could be damaging were you to take your eye off these contemporary issues for too long. I say "could" because it depends very much on the writer. God forgive that a poet should be obliged to be a politician.

AD: Especially in your early volumes, there can be observed an inclination towards – what seems to be on the surface at least – a politically/socially committed kind of poetry. Certain qualities of the work, such as sensitive representations of working-class existences in *Terry Street* (1969), historical dialogues of opposing social forces from the viewpoint of the oppressed in *Barbarians* (1979), descriptions of rural as well as industrial urban landscapes in various volumes, your admitted allegiance to industrial Clydeside, and other features prompted your description as a leftist poet well into the 1980s. How did you react to such – again, we can say – restrictive readings of your work then?

DD: I still find myself on the left side of the political spectrum in that I still hold to a belief in social justice. But to see me as that and only that kind of poet is restrictive or limiting, by which I mean, of course, that it's not how I see myself entirely. My book *Elegies* (1985), for example, isn't about Scotland although some of the poems are set there (as well as in Hull, and in a rural part of France, and in Dundee).

AD: You once wrote that "Community's a myth". In his review of *St. Kilda's Parliament* Anthony Thwaite suggests that an imaginative repossession of Scotland is taking place in your poetry. What is the role of imagination in the (re)creation of communal loyalties?

DD: Imagination is crucial to poetry and any other form of literature and art. In his masterpiece novel *Lanark* Alasdair Gray writes of Glasgow as an "unimagined" city, a city that for many years was somehow (or by and large) avoided by art. Even if there was much interest in art there Glasgow was rarely its subject. All that has changed and I'm convinced it's true of other parts of Scotland as well as of Glasgow.

From my own view of my work (which like any other writer's is unreliable) I feel that my "(re)creation" of communal loyalties occurs in some of my poems but in most of my short stories.

AD: The act of imagination is a key principle in your poetry, and it is perhaps more operative in your latest collection of poems, *Dante's Drum-kit*, than ever before. Can we see that volume as a landmark in the development of increasingly autonomous forms of representation in your poetry?

DD: It's not that I've tried deliberately to disengage myself from the political side of my poetry, but after the effort of writing *Elegies* I found what I had to say politically wearing a bit thin. There are poems of political consequence in *Northlight* (1988) and *Dante's Drum-kit* (1994) but on the whole I've been wary of that dimension of my writing, chiefly because I'm conscious of having reached a moment in my so-called career when self-parody or tedious repetition becomes a distinct possibility. I noticed this tendency in two older friends, the late Philip Larkin and the late Norman MacCaig, each of whom found himself becoming a caricature both physically and on the page and neither of whom enjoyed it. At my age (56) it's a good idea to try to stay new, if it can be managed; and if not, then a better idea to shut up and get on with something else.

I hope that the "act of imagination" is more conspicuous in my recent work. What I find, though, is that having published a book, I somehow, without deliberating it, make sure that the next book is different from its predecessor. I don't know why this happens.

AD: Where does the title of the book come from?

DD: Titles are always a problem for me. By *Dante's Drum-kit* I think I was drawing attention to the percussive side of poetic rhythm which is a bit loud in that volume. It was certainly an aspect of poetry I found myself fascinated by during the time I was writing the poems collected in that book. I could even have been drawing attention to the fact that I'd written a poem (in the book) in *terza rima*.

AD: In your criticism you have explicitly rejected art's complying with obligations other than those of inner convictions and aesthetic considerations. One of your premises about poetry is a demand for precision, meaning more than stylistic or semantic clarity. It signifies moral integrity, a capability of guileless responses to innermost impulses as well as an honest obedience to those impulses in representations of any kind of subject in verse. Is there a categorical imperative you think a poet should observe?

DD: All a poet is obliged to be is a poet. Once that's been accepted and digested, then the poet can be any sort of poet the poet needs to be – and I emphasize "need" and not "want". Just so long as the poet doesn't tell lies to himself or herself and try to use poetry for the purposes of the wide range of forms of special pleading on offer, the most common form of which is self-advertizing, then the freedom to be a poet should be infinite.

AD: Do you have any affinity with moral philosophy?

DD: I studied moral philosophy for a year when an undergraduate. I learned how to use expressions such as "that which" and spent a year unlearning them. I also worked as a secretary to my tutor, who was writing a book on the concept of liberty. He would dictate to me, I'd write it down in longhand, and then on a typewriter; and then I'd count the number of words. If there were more than twenty-six words in the sentence then it had to be revised until it was shorter. There could be no more words in a sentence than the letters of the alphabet. I asked him why, in a

book on the concept of liberty, he had to set himself this ridiculous unfreedom of sentences. He looked at me as if I were stupid. I looked at him as if he were stupid. We went on like that for weeks. It took him a very long time to pay me, and, in the meantime, I had to read his wife's poems. When he came round to my little house in *Terry Street* to give me the money he owed me, I was practising my clarinet – a florid but difficult study from a book of instruction and exercises by Klosé, I recall. He was horrified, and said I was wasting my time with "music" (pronounced like a dirty word) when I should be studying philosophy. Let my answer to your question be implied from the foregoing.

AD: To what extent is your *ars poetica* emotionally motivated?

DD: "Emotionally" is not the word I'd choose, although feeling is implicated in the ways in which I write. "Eccentric" could be better in that it includes the sense of emotion as well as individuality. As it happens, I'm fairly expert in my knowledge of written and published *ars poetica* and *art poetique* and so on. I'm fascinated by these things although I'm the first to admit that they don't help all that much when you come to put pen to paper. Writings like these are of the past, while one's own writing is of the present. No matter how much you know, or you think you know, the struggle is always with contemporary issues in aesthetics, and these are discovered in the act of writing, no matter what you're writing about, whether intimate, or political, or whatever.

AD: Do you agree with John Keats's opinion of poetry, who says that poetry should be "great and unobtrusive" and that it should not be "smokeable"?

DD: If I could smoke poetry I probably would, if only because I seem to have smoked just about everything else. "Great and unobtrusive" – very Keatsian. That would be nice.

AD: How is it possible to reconcile writing poetry with the duties of professorship?

DD: It's not always possible as much of my time is taken up with administration and teaching. Having said that, though, I seem to have written a lot during the past three or four years while I've been Head of the School of English at St Andrews, and Director of the St Andrews Scottish Studies Institute. This is repeating myself, or, rather, repeating Philip Larkin repeating himself, but you can only write a poem when you have a poem to write. Where life becomes frustrating is when I have a poem to write but at the same time a committee to attend, or a class of students to see, and the poem has to go on hold.

AD: What are you working on currently?

DD: I have a poem to write, and it's a long poem, of which I've completed around 115 pages so far. It's spoken by Eugene Politovsky, the Flag Engineer on the Russian fleet that sailed round the world to meet its destiny at the battle of Tsushima during the Russo-Japanese War. Part I was published in *Encounter* in 1983 under the title 'Politovsky's Letters Home' – the poem is in the form of Politovsky's letters to his wife. Since a few weeks ago, it's now called *The Donkey's Ears*, which is what Tsushima means in Japanese. It's about the beginning of the twentieth century as well as specific to its character. Historically, Politovsky wasn't a poet. He wasn't even much of a prose writer if translations of his letters (which were published in English) are anything to go by. I've made him a secret poet and overt engineer. Why I'm writing the poem is a mystery to me. What I'm clear about is that it's not a poem about Scotland, but about the world, and the hellish century which is about to become another century, indeed, a new millennium. And who knows how hellish that's going to be? I'm not ashamed of the fact that while Scotland is on the run-up to its first parliament since the early eighteenth century I'm writing a poem spoken by a Russian engineer who died at "the Trafalgar of the east" in May 1905. It doesn't faze me because I've written lots of other poems, some of which abut on present Scottish issues, but most of which don't. I'm incorrigible. I hope always to be truculent, obtuse, and incorrigible. My Muse demands of me that I have room for anything at all, for everything, the erotic and lyrical, the topical and political, the discursive and autobiographical, the main theme and the absolutely digressive, the very significant and the nursery rhyme. If there's anything I want as a poet, it's the stamina to maintain diversity and the response to what's necessary for my circumstances of writing.

DOUGLAS DUNN
EARLY HOURS IN DAIRSIE

2 follows 1, etcetera, night dusk,
Day dawn, and so we go, as Shakespeare says,
As syllables, a mere mumble of time.

A ghostly heron rises in the mist.
Three, four, five flaps, and then it vanishes
Into its own shroud-coloured featheriness.

Cool-clearing mist drifts on the sleepless stream
Then a high slit of July blue appears.
"Why are you here?" says the chattering water.

"Why are you here?" says the dawn chorus.
"You aren't walking a dog, or heading for work
In the fields, so why are you here at this

"Time by the Moonzie Burn at 5 A.M.?"
Do I need to explain, that I have come to see you,
And hear you? For you are beautiful,

And the weeds of water give off a cool scent
In these early hours, a fragrance of promises
Perfected by emergent, low sun.

I walked out to taste the freshness of summer.
Is that so suspicious? I like this bridge.
I am so very fond of you, this little strath,

With its burn, its high woodland to the west,
And far dew beginning to rise like smoke.
Who could refuse to get up from bed to walk

Among the cultivated peace of peace
Itself? I wouldn't call a country "mine".
But you are my country. You are birdsung;

You can do without my clumsy, human verse,
I know. Such sweetly chirupped cadences
Beat poetry into a cocked hat, but

I have to try at least to visit you
When you are at your best, in the cool dawn
Blending its moistures, sky showing through,

And should you find it smacks of loneliness,
I claim it's otherwise, and call it love,
My local and my universal kiss.

JAMES LASDUN
WOODSTOCK

Wudestoc: a clearing in the woods.
Forty miles from the town itself;
the name, as in Herzl's *Judenstaat*,
less about place than disclosure –
of a people, or an idea.

I was at prep school in Surrey at the time,
pre-pubescent; under my yearning eyes
the grounds – all greensward with copper beeches –
glimmered like the veil of heaven
about to be torn open.

At noon we stood on parade in divisions
and marched into lunch like soldiers.
The dining room
was painted with scenes from King Arthur.
Vividly out of green water a naked arm

Held a great shining sword . . .
In my first wet dream
Queen Guinevere seduced me in her tent.
There was an initiation rite:
six boys scragged you on the stony puntabout.

You were terrified but you wanted it.
Thereafter one had trouble with one's pronouns.
I found Queen Guinevere in the bed to my left.
Her name was Richard, I think, or Robert;
a cavalier to my roundhead,

or as one goy put it,
my jewnicorn.
Nightly my left arm crept between her sheets,
sneaking home in the small hours,
sticky with Guinevere's flowers.

We were like South Sea Islanders,
worshipping existence from afar
with our own cargo-cult
of whatever beached on our shore.
One boy found the empty sleeve

of *Electric Ladyland.*
We gazed till we felt the heavens opened
and the spirit like a dove descending;
Jimi and twenty-one naked girls,
Guineveres to a man;

Jimi in a braided military coat
and flower-power shirt;
a hawk-taloned dove
late of the 101st Airborne,
mouthing our cry of love.

I signed up for classical guitar
and plucked a lute-gentle twelve-bar blues
at our all-boys disco night
where the nursing sister briefly graced us,
sending her thanks and kisses on scented paper

which, in our excitement, we tore to pieces.
Later I bought an electric, though by that time
my left arm was half-numb
and the best people, Jimi included,
had checked out of the stadium.

I'm in Woodstock now,
on a mountain clearing,
my own *lichtung*
or niche in existence,
watching old footage of Woodstock.

Peace and Love . . . and War:
The throbbing choppers ferrying musicians
over the refugee traffic,
over the city-sized singalong
of Country Joe's "What are we fighting for?"

Pete Townsend in white jeans and braces
like one of Kubrick's droogies,
beating up his own axe;
Joe Cocker playing air-guitar, or is it
air-chainsaw, or air-bazooka?

Had I not seen this in a vision?
That record sleeve my tab of pure Owlsley;
vividly out of the lake the women rising,
bare-breasted, flower-strewn, Guineveres to a man;
Kesey's yippies frolicking in the mud –

A Mesopotamian puntabout;
Wavy Gravy offering to feed the multitude,
addressing them "listen, man . . ."
Too much already!
And after Max Yasgur's blessing,

Hendrix, amused-looking, laconic,
as in his Dick Cavett interview –
Cavett: "are you disciplined,
do you get up every morning and work?" And Jimi:
"well, I try to get up every morning . . ."

The long fringes on his sleeve
make eagle-wings as he sharpens his axe,
the usual left-handed Fender,
with its phallic arm
and womanly curves.

It was at Monterey, not here,
that he set fire to it on stage
after dry-humping an amp;
his instinct for sacrifice narrowing in
like Adam's in the Talmud,

his axe the *re'em* or one-horned ox
– a jewnicorn –
offered up to Jehovah.
I think of my left arm rising
vividly out of Lake Como,

slashed by a speedboat propellor
I'd summoned for the job
(of my hand didst thou require it)
of securing a right-handed future
righter-handed, that is,

which it did with the dexterity, ha-ha,
of a kosher butcher
removing the sciatic nerve
in honour of Jacob who lost his sciatic nerve
dry-humping an angel.

The water foamed red, red
as the mingling red chain-oil and flower-juices
of the blossoming red maples
I cleared from our meadow;
Guineveres to a man.

And vividly out of the water
the unsheathed sword of my own
startlingly white bone *And he said thy name*
between two labial flesh-flaps
shall no longer be called Jacob . . .

But Jimi, who still later could be said
to have offered up his own head
that we not forget to remember
the art not of getting somewhere
but of being there,

is in mellower fettle here. Calmly
he sharpens his curved axe –
Quat! hit clatered in the clyff as it cleve schulde,
for a few bursts of Machine Gun,
bringing the torso to his teeth,

a panther devouring a fawn,
our eagle-clawed dove
late of the 101ˢᵗ Airborne,
hybrid of lion and unicorn,
then with the dexterity

of a kosher *shohet*
or Saladdin with King Richard's handkerchief
or Sir Bertilak blooding Sir Gawain,
Bot here yow lakked a lyttel, sir
proceeds to slash apart

the Star-Spangled Banner,
bending the strings till they
carve through its flesh like the blades
(I will not let thee go except thou bless me)
of a speedboat propellor,

the bitten steel biting back
into his own flesh
which is our flesh,
just as the Star-Spangled Banner
is the blood-spangled heavens torn open

for the spirit like an F-105 Thunderchief descending
and the sound you hear is the sound
of something being annihilated
calmly, and for good.
And your name,

whatever it is,
is no longer what it was,
for as a prince
hast thou power with God and with men,
and hast prevailed.

TWO POEMS BY HARRY CLIFTON
ABOUT CHILDREN

At three on a winter afternoon
You reached out blindly, and snapped on the lamp,

And I saw, suddenly, how late it was
To be having this conversation. A streak of light

As thin as the minute-hand of a solar clock
Burned its way over the floor

From the great outdoors,
And for a moment, we hung in the middle realm

Between day and night. "This envelope"
You said, as you folded it twice for luck,

"Imagine it, as the shape of a human spine
In the earliest week...." And I saw it, an embryo

Setting out blindly, our mythic lines
Foreclosing around it, as the ancestors

Hovered, the living and the dead.
A million selves were crowding to a head

Inside me, each with its separate hope
Of not being nothing. And the unsaid

Broke through, with "How many years have we left?"
As that brilliant spoke of the sun

Shifted its allegiance, and was gone,
And the minute-hand moved on

For ever and ever. And over the floor
It spread, like something foretold –

The thinnest end of the wedge
Of absolute darkness, and of absolute cold.

A TALKING HEAD ON THE RUE DU BAC

"I can't go on. I'll go on."
                    Samuel Beckett, 'The Unnameable'

As I staggered into the Rue du Bac
The heavens opened. In the zinc bars
Drinkers paused. Outside, police
Took shelter in nearby doors,
And I thought of Giacometti,
Legless on a mantelpiece,
Or Beckett's talking head in a jar,

Who would give the best of themselves
For an hour of conversation,
A blue streak, an unstoppable jag,
Incontinent, shattering
Plateglass windows, Sevres delph,
Like a man on a drunken batter.
Metros spun their monologues

Underground. I closed my eyes
A moment, to clear my head
Of vodka and foie gras,
Of oysters bedded in ice,
And heard the swish of Michelin treads,
The bicycles, stilettos pass.
And blinked again. I was not dead,

Just following the curve of the world
In my own small way,
Rambling on, with nothing to say,
From shelter to shelter. Soon, a quai
Would show itself, round the next bend.
For no good reason, pretty girls
And the stone statue of Chateaubriand

Leapt, like improvisation,
Into the picture. Pedalling
Hard, another Molloy
Downwind of his destination,
Dressed in dickybow, held an umbrella
Overhead, as he wobbled away.
Our Lady of the Miraculous Medal

Chimed, just once. I saw, I heard,
At the heart of desperate cheerfulness,
Not spirit, not the Word,
But winking neon, blues and greens,
A brilliant pharmaceutical cross,
The tricorned hats of Etamine's,
The profit and the loss.

And suddenly, there it was, the Seine –
A street the length of a cloudburst
Or a song on an underground train
From station to station, falling away
To the dry heaves, to yellow bile,
To the cold water of rainswept quais.
Bloodshot, from a night on the tiles,

Others besides myself, in straits,
Were waiting for the skies to break,
And whistling in the dark –
Alcoholics with the shakes,
Bearded tramps, their flies undone,
Accusing heaven. Early or late?
I no longer knew. But I had to go on.

CAROLE SATYAMURTI
IMPERIAL

More and more, I notice yellow.

The way it stands against the dark,
rescuing brown from black, for instance.
The shapes the pen makes, writing yellow.
The shapes the mouth makes, saying yellow,
yellow.., the way, even repeated, it resists inanity.

It is what stops the whole leafy, grassy world
from being blue as the sky, and boring.

Of course, there's jaundice, sulphur, fever, wasps,
but consider the vast swatch of natural pleasures:
the brimstone of butterflies, a blackbird's beak,
the heart of a marguerite, to be but arbitrary.

It is the colour of wealth – grain and honey,
saffron, amber, tiger's eye – and sharp, sad lemons.
How sinister and gorgeous are the words for it,
delicious in the mouth – gamboge, massicot,
xanthin, luteolin, orpiment, cadmium, weld.

In an imagined room I have three vases,
Qing, spirited from the Metropolitan Museum,
their different shapes, yellows, singing to each other;

and, from the Top Kapi Palace, a small plain bowl
most beautiful of all the Sultan's treasure
deep, buttery perfection of its glaze
soul of balance, lustre of joy
Imperial Yellow.

KWAME DAWES
FROM: MID-LAND

VII: EPOCH

"I moan this way 'cause he's dead", she said.
"Then tell me, who is that laughing upstairs?"
"Them's my sons. They glad."

Ralph Ellison, Invisible Man

An epoch glows beneath her skin. This near woman.
Her nose spreads like flattened clay, her lips
Bloody grapefruit: wet, startled crimson.
Her makeup betrays haste, the base too pale for her
Fingers. She has no time for the paletting,
The mixing of hues to find the dialect
Of her history. There is the epoch of silence
In her skin, something hidden, something
Like a curse in the long of her lower back
Before the defiant cockiness of her buttocks.
A family of tangerine people; they are black.
Thoroughly African, southern folks,
With slave songs like the Jews,

Laws dangling on their foreheads.
Yet a family shaped in the kerosene smelling
Back quarters, where old pork was cured; at night
The flies, groggy, drunk with the heat
And Buddy Lawrence panting into this soil, this flesh,
This tendon tight woman, suddenly making
Babies, making a narrative of people's blood ties.

Powie, she was given no other name.
Still, she had the exotic wit to whisper
"Alma" into the pale skin of her false-eyed
Child. They christened her "Alma"
In the Baptist Church, such pure natural
Light on her transparent skin and hair.

In Greeleyville the corn leaves
Rustle; a yellowed parchment of pain.
No one talks of the furtive wetness
Of the sex in the dark time, no one admits it.
So she sits here; generations beyond
Wondering at the anger beneath the skin,
The wailing stone of stumbling, the piled
Rocks upon the heads of the living and the dead.

Powie begat Alma begat Okia begat Lynne begat Krystal,
The years do not seem enough between the ash and tar
Of a Sumter lynching and the promise of better days.
Her skin does not trust its language
Of appeasement, the whisper of atonement.
She stands in the stark sun, longing to darken
The skin, but it grows transparent
In the heat, and all is palimpsest, the language
Of the blood under the skin.

ROBERTO MUSSAPI
THE SPLENDOUR OF THE DARK

And evening came down like someone who's going away
taking beyond the door the extreme dazzle
of the corridor, leaving the smell of coldness
beyond the adored and still uncrossed threshold
where in the morning with the first rays of gold
the wife came through stepping like a fairy
interrupting the waterclock, waking up the hours,
moving among the windows as if in a swimming-pool.

There, beyond the barrier now quite dark,
where desire is grown and dreams are put together,
hedge upon hedge the eye stares at each evening,
in the harsh borderland between the region of darkness
and the last smell of the familiar grass,
repressing the nostalgia of the repeated

distant goodbye, where the flower of dreams grows back,
in the dark which little by little begins to shine
on the forgetful streams – remembered by the heart –
when in the room in silence a glass glimmers
and sleep nourishes the glowing memory.

Translated from the Italian by Alistair Elliot

RITA ANN HIGGINS
THE CLEMSON EXPERIENCE

*(Conference of Irish Studies. Conference centre
surrounded by golf course, formerly a plantation)*

In the Walker Golf Course where no one walked
Joyce's wet dreams were splashed about
in the name of the father.
Carson's bullets slip-jigged and reeled
Yeats' black habits were boiled and peeled
more Joyce dot com for psycho netters
Joyce in Celluloid, Joyce in hotpants
Joyce in toilet with betters.

Heaney's bogmen were dragged up
by their rotting stubs
their bones picked asunder
the contents of their ancient bellies
made flesh and flung amongst us
on this golf course at Clemson, once a plantation
where tailgating is something dirty Yeats didn't do.

The golfers over-the-hilled it at 8am
in their twenties, in their trolleys, off their trolleys
on their starters orders.

The man with the megaphone threw shapes.
"Proper golf attire does not include
grown men with big bellies prancing round
this 18 hole in suspender belts
shorts should be of Bermuda persuasion
not to the shins or below
not too far above the knees
no balls in the trees
that last remark was a slip of the tongue.

Right you cock shots, you hot shots
only collared shirts here
shiftless losers over there
no flashy ankle socks with tiger paws or other
absolutely no swim wear, no Aran sweaters
if you want Synge try Ballroom four."

Papers about what Jack B did to Lady G
while W.B. was exorcising his tea
or viewing 'A Portrait' from his tightest orifice (with slides)
chaired by a Carolina Panther supporter from Chattanooga
or the pitying shape of Irish drama
as told through the space invaders in Friel's work
or learning the quotable Yeats and Heaney in three easy lessons
for after dinner speeches or the odd peace process.

Megaphoner-all-aloner was losing it with the golfers.

"Hey you, Mr. Inappropriate chest of drawers
do you want me to send you in there
where they pick Heaney, poke Joyce
pickle the bones from man of ice
O.D. on Yeats and queer theory
Tiresias and Art O' Leary.

Where all day is spent finding the missing link
between Behan, Boland and Lewinsky.
And you with the black leggings
put your hand on your affliction
when I am dressing you down.

This is Clemson, home of The Clemson Tigers
where the Blue Ridge Mountains shield you
from the smell of that rotting cheese
where Lake Heartwell ducks eat gluten-free bread
where the azaleas and camellias
would sicken a sorry dog with that splash of colour
where the chrysanthemums are edging in just for notice.

The choice is yours, will you wear proper golfing attire
or will I let the wind-filled professors at you?
Where they Heaney time by plucking the maggots
and sucking the marrow out the bones of the bogmen of Ireland
on this championship golf course, once a plantation.
What's it to be, you in the girl's knickers !"

PETER BLAND
THE OLD PLACE

Any minute now, round the next corner,
past the parachute factory and the shunting yards,
we'll be there. It's not been easy
travelling backwards, walking blind,
everyone yelling "Put out those lights",
but I needed to show you this bombed-out landscape
and meet some old ghosts. Look, there they are
on a front step scrubbed white as chalk,
smart army fatherman, and motherwoman
in her factory turban and red Spanish shawl.
Now they're waving. You see, I'm forgiven
for being born when they were old,
for crowding out their wartime meetings,
for knowing that home was only bed-and-board.
Come in! All are welcome. I'm the prodigal returning.
Share their bread and these boiled-up bones,
hear dead dogs barking and the gramophone playing
'Bye Bye Blackbird' and 'One Alone'.
Didn't I mention the endless party
waiting for the All Clear at the back of their minds?
Didn't I say how they lived through hard times
angry but never drab? Never mind. See
how they smile as we hurry towards them
to hear their tall stories and pour out the wine.

PETER REDGROVE

SNAKEHOUSE, COOL CHURCH AND INSECT FARM

Here I am in the snakehouse and insect-farm
At this moment having touched
A sinewy resident and been astonished
That the serpent-skin was dry cool and muscular,
And how after touching, my hand smelled sweet,
Like beeswax-polished balustrades, like honey.

What happiness to know
That women are free now
To bless the bread and wine
In the great empty
And sunny churches,

And what further happiness, a step merely
If she bared herself to the waist
And plunged her arms into the basket of snakes
And lifted them up and offered them
In two hissing heavy handfuls for her sacrament,
Woman and snake smelling identically sweet,
Woman and snakes in the same sibilance.

The zipper-legged giant centipede
Paused in his hundredfold walk
Polished as candlesticks, cool as a canteen of cutlery;
The bird-swallowing spider ventilated in,
High-heeled hoofs tiptoed lightly
As a black soufflé, bouffant
Down my dancetty forearm;

That first cool touch of toads – enlightenment!

CONNIE BENSLEY
SANATORIUM
Norfolk 1955

A dozen people have driven up to see me
this summer – Ratty, the Zieglers, Pixie and so on.
They tour the Norfolk churches, then come on here.
We have tea in my room: they bring cake
and I do imitations of the nurses.
We have a convivial time, but I finally wilt
under the pressure to be entertaining.
Patients must be entertaining, or who will visit them?

And it's difficult to find space for them, my room
is so untidy. Even the bedside table is deplorable:
yesterday's ashtray unemptied, yesterday's *Times* unread,
the foul-tasting agar-agar which I don't now need
thanks to the laxative effect of P.A.S.,
the mirror for shaving, the extra socks (no heating
until October), my blue silk spotted scarf,
two boxes of Marcovitch, a file marked 'TO DO, May 12'.

Charlie, the male nurse, has just turned up
to take last night's bottle, followed by Mrs May
for the hoovering. She skirts the thunderbox
and tells me she's going to see her daughter
in America next month on the Queen Mary (£120 return,
she's saved up). I'm on my best behaviour with Mrs M.
because she once told me I looked like
Rex Harrison. I felt much better that day.

Some people send me improving books (perhaps they think
there's time for a quick conversion) – books about
Billy Graham and Ouspensky, books on Christianity
and Being Saved. This seems ominous, and rather a cheek.
But I do find that thinking, even for short spells,
is interesting. I've taken to doing it in the morning
when they bring the tea, but not for more than
ten minutes, with no mind-wandering allowed.

This week I'm thinking about Buddhism,
one of the eight-fold paths each day.
I look forward to seeing the effect
after a month. One thing I've already noticed
is that other people's actions are often
frightfully wrong. I ponder this over breakfast –
brassy tea, toast like linoleum, a dispirited egg,
two sachets of P.A.S. which I force down;

and now here comes the shopper; a German girl,
married to the thoracoplasty in room 49. I ask
for chocolate and writing paper, and she takes £1
from my wallet. This is kept in the fruit bowl,
on top of the spare bulb which I inherited from
the cordial de Musset, who had room 8.
He used it to keep his terrapins warm. I wonder
what became of them. But I don't want to ask.

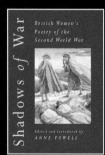
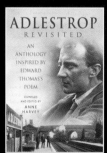

ROBERT SAXTON

AGAINST VENICE
after Marinetti, 8th July 1910

Old Venice: sick queen who won't abdicate.
In your prime we loved you. Mosquito-blown,
You maunder, centuries past your sell-by date,
Rheumatic aches in every crumbling stone.
The waves break up the flotsam of your throne
In a gold haze burned off a sun-scorched sea.
You sink, like a seaweed wreath, with a soft moan
Darkwards. Still they drape you in festivity,
Soul-pox, lanterns at dawn, love-duel on bended knee.

Your bed has been unsprung by caravans
Of lovers. Veiled, they linger a few weeks
Round the porch of the Temple of the Glans,
Then, crazed, burst in at last, with molten cheeks.
Levantines, Turks, Egyptians, Cockneys, Greeks
Crowd the Rialto with the worst of news,
Their worm-infected passions and antiques
All counterfeit. St Mark's hypoteneuse
Tinkles its triangle in adulterous ooze.

Nurses of the saddest sanatorium
In the world, Venetians awake! You doze
In fake moonshine. Dash the ciborium
To the ground, smash all the Doge's windows
To let in the future, scrape the Tiepolos
Off the ceiling. Gondoliers, abjure your oars!
Stop digging graves in a swamp. Evolve, dodos!
Cease your rocking-chair rides for cretins and whores
In your beribboned hats and stripy pinafores.

Like the sister of some grand contralto,
Venice, superfluous, reclines inert.
Sound the reveille! Blow the Rialto
Sky-high! Sneak a large bomb beneath her skirt
And watch the shadowy queen turn extrovert.
Pave the Cloaca Maxima. A new empire
Of electric light dawns. Admit the spurt
Of trains, sensuous speed: shock the arriving choir-
Master in snow-blue beard and Tyrolean attire.

Venice, don't let those bullies force your nose
Underwater – churchmen, poets, dead-eyed
Pimps, Ruskin's ghost whose touch can decompose,
The stench of half a million words. This tide
Will turn when the hero comes to win you, bride –
Brave engineer whose howitzers will plume
Your bed, whose giant bridges will bestride
Your lagoon like gymnasts, vaulting from tomb
To tomb in a glitter of knives. Bride, meet your groom.

JAYANTA MAHAPATRA
A PASTORAL PERHAPS

By the scummy pond, in the thin rain,
a woman shakes her hair loose,
before entering the water. Through the grove
of bamboos dripping bright raindrops,
a long abandoned thought appears to push a smile
at her lips. Audacious shadows open
to take her in; she shrugs, strong, unaware.

Leaves green, sway under the cloudy sky,
and only the woman's sunbronzed face looks out
above the water. The air drops quietly back into the past,
a part of the present seems to break away.
The destiny of India heaves in darkness,
in the memory of ancient waters.
In spite of itself, the banks smile back at her.

All we do is demand something for ourselves.
From a place not ours,
or from the immodesty of a woman bathing,
perhaps from the thought of God's sacred ground.
To strip the wind off the hills, and gather
fruit for the dance. Our need is a cruel ghost,
for whom we long for our strength, and wait for
strangely in the heart's many dark empty rooms.

FRED VOSS

EXACTLY WHAT IT IS AND DOES

I love the black and red sides of freighter ships
with 20-foot-high cranes sticking up out of them
and the fists of men
around tool steel wrenches they have worn smooth
with their flesh and 30 years of straining
with every muscle in their body to tighten big steel nuts down so tight
they squeal
I love the wheels of old factory carts
with their sheet metal tops so dented and scratched and bent and ugly
with the million loads
they have rolled across concrete or asphalt
and I love the gift
of a day to fill with sweating with arms
wrapped around crane chains
and filthy 1-ton bars of steel and the spindles
of old machines still whirring smoothly at 1,000 rpm
I love the loud colors on the sides of trucks
racing down freeways toward loading docks
and everything that is nothing more
than exactly what it is
and does
axles and engines of great trucks idling beside gas pumps with the heat
radiating up out of their hoods and smokestacks at
the crack of dawn
and a 3/4-inch tap dripping with bright red cutting oil
as it slices the threads into the inside of the steel tube
and the old man
so good
he can turn any metal into any part on any machine
beginning to teach
the young man
all he knows so that the young man's child
will never go hungry.

THE REVIEW PAGES

Inside the Cyclotron

HARRY CLIFTON ON THE HARDY–HANNAH LINE

**The Harvill Book of
Twentieth Century Poetry in English**
Edited by Michael Schmidt
Harvill, £20
ISBN 1 86046 351 7

IF CHRIST, AS Gerard Hopkins wrote, is the only true literary critic, then God, I suspect, is going to be the only true anthologist of the twentieth century. God being dead, though, as the continental philosophers tell us, a second-best option has had to emerge, in the shape of partial anthologies edited by those who profess to be at war with each other while sharing a liberal humanist mindset that unites rather than divides them. Approximations, in a word, which taken together, may add up to some kind of general picture.

Michael Schmidt, before delivering his anthology, has clearly been watching the trends and counter-trends of the last twelve months, and wants to be something else again. No word, therefore, of social let alone religious-philosophical contextualising in his Introduction. And no biographical details at the back. In his own words, no "poets" only "poems", whirling about like atoms in a huge experimental cyclotron called Modernism – acting, interacting and most especially reacting (a favourite word) to each other. And lest all that seem too anti-traditional, he is anxious to bracket the whole gravitational dance with two acts of language that establish, or re-establish, a more conventional continuity between the pre-modern and the post-modern. Here is a stanza from his opening poem, Thomas Hardy's 'Darkling Thrush':

> At once a voice arose among
>   The bleak twigs overhead
> In a full-hearted evensong
>   Of joy illimited;
> An aged thrush, frail, gaunt and small,
>   In blast-beruffled plume,
> Had chosen thus to fling his soul

Upon the growing gloom.

And here is another one, from Sophie Hannah's 'The Norbert Dentressangle Van', specially commissioned to close the book on a metrical-stanzaic echo of its opening, and by implication to show the continuing vitality of traditional form:

> I sketch my evening like a plan.
> I think I recognise
> The Norbert Dentressangle van…
>   That mine are clouded eyes…
> say whiteness, whiteness, that's the shade…
>   That paint is tins apart
> might mean some progress can be made
> in worlds outside the heart.

Cynical hindsight might see that thrush, a few years later, dropping dead of mustard gas off a Flanders branch, or the van on its way to the heart of London with something other than cans of paint. But that would be history, and Schmidt is less interested in history than in stylistics, the innate optimism of achieved poetic form. Insanity, collective or individual, might supervene for a while, but the thrush will sing again, the van bring back an everyday pattern and reason reassert itself. The form-creating impulse, this book seems to be saying, will survive anything chaos can throw at it.

That stoical, reasonable attitude some might class as peculiarly Anglo-Saxon, a luxury that the rest of Europe with its irreversible brokenness of poetic form, could ill afford. In this connection, it is worth going back to the man Schmidt takes as his model, anthologist Michael Roberts, whose *Faber Book of Modern Verse* appeared in 1936. Like Schmidt, Roberts is inclined to insist, sometimes to the point of pedantry, on the technical rather that the visionary, but he does at least make a space for what he calls the "European" poet, that is, the poet writing in English whose work is clearly informed by a sense of Western crisis, be it social or religious-philosophical or both at the same time. Yeats and

POETRY REVIEW

56

Eliot are, of course, the exemplars, with huge American off-shoots in the order-and-chaos explorations of Wallace Stevens and the desperate leap of faith in jazz age technology that is Hart Crane's 'The Bridge'.

> O sleepless as the river under thee,
> Vaulting the sea, the prairies' dreaming sod,
> Unto the lowliest sometime sweep, descend
> And of the curveship lend a myth to God.

Schmidt, on the other hand, wants little to do with "poetry's context, its usefulness, its witness and moral probity construed in the light of the age's shifting preferences and concerns", as he makes abundantly clear in his Introduction, preferring us, it would seem, to read these poets as interfacings of Modernism with late Romanticism. So although they are respectfully represented – no more so, and at times less so, that the more Anglo-Saxon Thomas Hardy, Rudyard Kipling, Edward Thomas, Donald Davie, Philip Larkin et al – they are never allowed to set the tone.

A clue to all this is provided by Schmidt's own *Lives of the Poets*, in many ways the true introduction to this anthology (the actual Introduction is drawn, verbatim at times, from parts of that text). There, a line of poets who might be described, in their different ways, as visionary, from Yeats to Dylan Thomas and David Gascoyne, through to Allen Ginsberg and Ted Hughes, is subjected to largely unsympathetic readings, in which their sacramental concerns – sometimes misdescribed as Romanticism – are subtly discredited, at times by co-opting biographical detail (Allen Ginsberg signing the papers for his mother's lobotomy), or made out to be morally questionable (Ted Hughes' "sentimentality of violence"). At the same time, a counter-strain of poets who were or are against the grain of contemporary excesses, who cleanse the idiom and restore measure, be they H. D. against the Georgians, William Empson against the Thirties political poets, Donald Davie against the

Dylan Thomas romantics or Yvor Winters against the Eliot-Crane Jazz-Age disintegrations, are restored to grace. The critical lexicon employed is liberal humanist, psychology-based, committed to cause and effect. No trace here of the Blakean-Swedenborgian-Manichean historical demonology of that great translated Other, Czeslaw Milosz. As a reading of the century, not everyone will agree with it, but it is presented with a huge internal consistency, in both volumes.

All anthologies are good anthologies in at least one sense – they bring over, from the insider realm to the so-called general reader in the middle ground (literally and figuratively) of bookshops, a body of work that might otherwise have sat unread on the poetry shelves. Given that one such anthology may be all the poetry many homes will ever possess, the editorial pitch of the Introduction can be crucial. Wooing the consumer with anxious-to-please blandishments or the rhetoric of "accessibility" is not Schmidt's way, but there is a danger, which he doesn't entirely avoid, of going too far in the opposite direction. At times I felt he had forgotten the less-informed reader altogether while busily engaging the rest of us – the poets, critics, reviewers – in a high level discussion of Modernist aesthetics, as the forgotten reader, peering through a crack in the seminar door, quietly closed it and moved on.

Michael Schmidt has not been slow to criticise the approaches of other anthologists in the recent past, and his Introduction hearkens back to Philip Larkin's *Oxford Book of Twentieth Century Poetry* as an origin of the omni-tolerant or "democratic" tendency he abhors. Of Larkin, however, it can at least be said that he sat up there in Oxford for two terms prior to his anthology, just reading. As Schmidt's is the fourth large anthology to roll off the presses in less than a year, an obvious question suggests itself. To what extent are these anthologists enlarging the scope of their own reading, exploring beyond their normal ambits, between, say, the acceptance of a proposal and the eventual submission of the MSS? To what extent, pressured by the accelerated publishing schedules and Millennium fever, are they falling back on "unexcludables", borrowings from other anthologies where the groundwork may also not have been done, and whatever happens to be within their editorial field of vision at the time? In Schmidt's case, the question is prompted by the large preponderance of poets from his own Carcanet list, the more modest of whom will be as surprised as I was to find themselves elevated to twentieth-century representative status (albeit as "poems" rather than as "poets") though the rest, of course, will think it no more than they deserved at the very outset. I doubt, however, that the large number of obvious omissions from Ireland, Britain, America and Australia who happen to publish elsewhere than Carcanet Press will see it in quite the same light.

In a reading of the century which begins with Hardy and ends with a Hardyesque echo, it is worth remembering Hardy himself. As a poet with a novelist's eye for psychological nuance, whose tight forms hold his emotions in check, his presiding spirit is entirely consistent with the quiet epiphanies that run like a spine through this anthology, from John Crowe Ransom and Edna Millay, through Gwen Harwood, C. H. Sisson and Donald Davie to Eavan Boland, Louise Glück, Gwyneth Lewis and Sophie Hannah, with many others along the way. On the negative side, as Davie has pointed out, Hardy may also be responsible for an emotional repression within English poetry of the century, a

tendency, as he puts it in his well-known 'Remembering the Thirties', for quietness to become quietism:

> A neutral tone is nowadays preferred.
> And yet it may be better, if we must,
> To praise a stance impressive and absurd
> Than not to see the hero for the dust.

I would add that Hardy's sheer technical facility, even when applied to nothing in particular, may prefigure the millions of manufactured poems this century whose "percentage of felt experience", in Czesław Miłosz's phrase, is extremely low. It has to be said, as one gets towards the end of this hugely readable book, that the manufactured tends to triumph over the felt.

First came Pound, at the turn of the century, an American anxious to teach the Old World the gospel of Modernism. Then came Schmidt himself, an American anxious to learn from the Old World reactions to Modernism. Modernism and its reactions – that is the force-field drawing together the disparate material in this anthology. Definitive it certainly isn't, and flawed it may be by editorial *lèse majesté*, but Schmidt is prepared to stand over his approach ("inclusions and exclusions are generally deliberate") and take the rap. As for the general reader, hovering out there between the various texts, will he or she opt for Modernism or Social Context? Well, as Philip Larkin puts it in 'The Old Fools', we shall find out.

Lecture Notes and Scraps of Meat

by Kevan Johnson

ANNE CARSON

Autobiography of Red
Cape, £10
ISBN 0 224 05973 4

'HERO KILLS MONSTER' would be an obvious headline for the original myth of Geryon, a winged

red monster, and the mighty Herakles (Hercules) who slays him as part of his famous labours. Stesichoros, the post-Homeric Greek poet, departed from tradition by telling the tale from the monster's point of view – a narrative trajectory which Anne Carson also traces in *Autobiography of Red*. Carson is a classics professor in Montreal, but she's not content to simply show off her knowledge. What she offers is a dynamic rewrite of the story, a sharp modernisation which nonetheless draws from a deep well of myth. As a synopsis of her own book – subtitled "A novel in verse" – the following preface is perfect: "...the fragments of the *Geryoneis* read as if Stesichoros had composed a substantial narrative then ripped it to pieces and buried the pieces in a box with some song lyrics and lecture notes and scraps of meat".

The opening chapters simulate a childish simplicity. I found myself pulling faces at the unalloyed winsomeness of lines such as "When Geryon was little he loved to sleep but even more he loved to wake up. / He would run outside in his pajamas". (I bet be would, the little tyke.) But throughout the book, styles and subjects constantly interbreed, making new shapes. A study of the game of marbles, which considers the relative value of a "cat's-eye" and a "steelie", gets mixed up with bouts of not altogether consensual sexual fumblings between brothers and then, without warning, gives birth to this extraordinarily potent sentence: "Voyaging into the rotten ruby of the night became a contest of freedom and bad logic" – a little masterpiece, in my opinion.

Anne Carson has either a very good memory or a terribly accurate imagination; her version of childhood is wonderfully truthful. The intermittent tremors, both pleasurable and awful, the aggressive and affectionate politics of early family life, the sense of a world outside – incomprehensible but not necessarily unfriendly. Sometimes Carson sets up a plain tableau (a table, two chairs) and then opens up the window with an inspirational image. For example: "Geryon and his mother had supper alone. / They grinned at each other *as night climbed ashore*" (my italics).

Geryon's childhood lasts just long enough. Any longer and it would be difficult to shake off the idea of the protagonist as a cute bunny, albeit one with serious intellectual aspirations and a future appointment with Mr Freud's couch. But before his dysfunctional tics begin to irritate, Carson changes focus, switching to what is actually the heart of her fictional history:

> Then he met Herakles and the kingdoms of his life
> all shifted down a few notches.
> They were two superior eels
> at the bottom of the tank and they recognised each
> other like italics.

The boy-meets-boy love affair is poignantly written. Geryon is prey to a disorienting intoxication. It leaves the rest of his life utterly empty, and he vacillates between amorous intensity and general ennui. Young love has often been eulogised, but seldom does a writer catch the element of teenage gaucherie which is intrinsic to it. Carson manages it beautifully – "He had nothing to say to anyone. He felt loose and shiny. / He burned in the presence of his

mother". She perceptively identifies a certain wistfulness at the raging of the boy's own hormones: "Love does not / make me gentle or kind, thought Geryon".

At times the monster and his hero are just... well – a couple of kids, groping for something. In this extract, the poetry thrives in the cracks between inarticulate mutterings and eloquent description:

> *I guess I'm someone who will never be satisfied*,
> said Herakles. Geryon felt all nerves in him move to
> the surface of his body.
> *What do you mean satisfied?*
> *Just – satisfied. I don't know.* From far down the
> freeway came a sound
> of fishhooks scraping the bottom of the world.
> *You know. Satisfied.* Geryon was thinking hard.
> Fires twisted through him.

There are glinting particulars in this collection, but just as often its net effect depends upon novelistic aggregation of detail. Although photography is one of its main subjects, its method is more strictly cinematic. We are rarely afforded lyric snapshots, but regularly find ourselves situated in the middle of a scene – implicated in time (another central theme). I confess that while I appreciated her brick-by-brick structuring I was constantly on the lookout for a more urgent poetic thrill. There are no stanzas in *Autobiography of Red*, commas are uncommon, and the enjambment is generally without significance – to be severe, one could complain that the poetry *lacks silence*. But it's evident that background and build-up are very much part of the action-plan. In 'XVII. She', we get half a dozen lines of chit and chat before Geryon reaches the bedroom of Herakles' mother and hits the light switch – then suddenly "the room sprang towards him with its unappeasable debris of woman liquors". It's the kind of line that stops you reading, while you stare into space for a little while...

The end of Geryon and Herakles' romantic misadventure occurs midway through the book, which then proceeds to trail off conspicuously. Plot is foregrounded and a degree of linguistic intensity is lost. The Lad in Red works in a library, travels to Buenos Aires, studies German philosophy and hangs out in street cafes and lecture halls; there is much talk of ancient law codes, scepticism, the price of a double espresso, and Pascal. In effect, Geryon turns into an existentialist anti-hero – a young man adrift in a strange city, questioning his own reality in the horrid solitude of his hotel room. But there are better versions of this genre already published, and contextually it pales beside the unique intrigue of pages 1-71. Later memorable passages tend to hark back to the pre-Argentinian epoch – especially to adolescence, when serious questions could still be asked in good faith. Thinking of "the noise that colours make", he mentally flicks back the pages to a 7th Grade science project recalling: "Most / of those he interviewed had to admit they did not hear / the cries of roses / being burned alive in the noonday sun. *Like horses*, Geryon would say helpfully, / *like horses in war*". Mysterious, but I have a strange feeling that I know what he means.

Autobiography of Red is not exactly kaleidoscopic (its favourite colour is definitely between pink and purple) but its expressive spectrum is deeply impressive. Carson has come up with a style which can happily incorporate a wide range of different discourses; her book is, in the truest sense, multicultural. It revisits an area explored in 'The Glass Essay', the outstanding poem in her previous collection, *Glass and God*: the connections and disconnections between personal intimacies and biography, poetry and history. Are monster and hero alter-egos? To what extent is one's life narratable? Is the self a myth? Like any substantial writer, Anne Carson causes her readers to wonder...

Cutting the Mustard

by Paul Groves

ROBERT MINHINNICK

Selected Poems

Carcanet, £6.95
ISBN 1 85754 383 1

ROBERT MINHINNICK WAS born in 1952 in Neath. His *Selected Poems* press release says he focuses on "not just ozone layers and rainforests but a whole vision tying together ecology, culture and human values in a pattern of renewal and vitality". This claim is not matched by the book's contents, which predominantly treat of his Welsh background and environment. Ecology, no. Plants, yes. Throughout 128 pages we get bladderwrack, bracken, broom, bryony, cactus, dandelion, elderflower, helleborine, hibiscus, hogweed, honeysuckle, hydrangea, iris, lichen, lily, nettle, orchid, ragwort, rhododendron, samphire, sea rocket, stitchwort, vine, and yucca. An adverse criticism? Far from it. His abundant vegetation is not some overcrowded Edwardian garden but natural phenomena unsentimentally presented. He said of his anthologised material in *The Bright Field* (Carcanet, 1991): "I hope there is no sentimentality in this writing". His hope is confirmed. It comes closer to the toughness of Ted Hughes than to the

tweeness of Patience Strong. For him, a plant is almost mystically elemental and quite unlike manmade constructs. Unlovely urban backwaters are evoked in passing, not with tub-thumping venom but resignation. These poems are not eco-political tracts: they are the musings of a man confronting his confusing century with Victorian painterly precision.

The eighteenth-century Swedish botanist Linnaeus swooned in ecstatic wonder at his first sight of gorse in bloom on Wimbledon Common: in 'The Ice Tower' Minhinnick gives us "One June evening, the gorse / Ecstatic as goldfinches" without indicating that he knows the anecdote. The image is strikingly exact. Similarly, he depicts a former politician thus: "I saw Enoch Powell once, tiny, / Squat as a goshawk, shaking / With rage as he described a plot / That had done him down". Was the wizened rightwinger ever more economically described? And there is something uncommonly apt about his portrayal of flora in 'from *Breaking Down*': "a circle / Of foxgloves, tall, wizard-like".

Minhinnick is no stranger to wizardry, not because he embraces occultism (he doesn't) but because his penetrating gaze can deconstruct his surroundings with otherworldly aplomb. This brings him close to Martian exposition in such poems as 'The Verger' with its intensity and pinpoint accuracy. Elsewhere, we are brought up short by "the hymen of a coffee jar" and a tropical moth with "wings like two South Americas" and – in a celebrated poem, 'The Looters', about the results of a prolonged blizzard – "Abandoned on the motorway / The container lorries are dislocated / Vertebrae".

Minhinnick takes risks with language because he knows he can get away with them. Even his least felicitous description (in 'Old Ships', among the earliest pieces here) – "from mammary Glamorgan" – is salvaged by the next line: "To the stamp-album countries". His way with metaphor is rarely strained and often surprising. Among titles from the seventies the touch is not always assured, though poems like 'Ivy' show that at a comparatively young age he could write particularly well.

Demerits? "I am told sometimes that there is obscurity [in my work]" he has said. Correct, but not a debilitating amount. In 'Bronze Age' the approach is too private and meditative to appeal to a wide audience, and it is therefore less successful than 'Ghost Train', which immediately precedes it. 'The Aerial' is an uneasy blend of rhyme and free verse, which reads ABAB for two stanzas, AABB for one stanza, and nothing so formally structured thereafter. In 'The Swimming Lesson' he says "they had swam". These inconsistencies should not detract from a formidable corpus which, even now, shows its author developing.

Minhinnick's travel writing has taken him far afield, refreshing his vocabulary and energising his ability in delightful and promising ways. He has yet to write his best verse. Wearing the garb of World Citizen rather than Porthcawl denizen is the way ahead. Too many Welsh poets are hoist with their own petard, ranting on defensively about what it is to be a full-blooded Celt in the modern world. Minhinnick's poetry avoids this trap, though only just. We can, hopefully, look forward to more various examples of his art, as in the haiku 'Newark': "Latest *Rolling Stone*. / Pitcher of Budweiser. / I think I could live here". Blake Morrison noted in the *New Statesman*, about Christopher Reid's first book: "After reading *Arcadia* you feel that the world is a stronger, richer, more various place than you'd supposed", a comment which certainly applies to the less-highly-rated but equally-deserving Minhinnick.

Mysterious Company

by Hugh Macpherson

Skating on the Sea: Poetry from Finland

Edited and translated by Keith Bosley
Bloodaxe £10.95
ISBN 1 85224 388 0

BOTH BLOODAXE BOOKS and Keith Bosley have already done fine work in bringing Finnish poetry to us. Bloodaxe have published two other anthologies, and individual books by Edith Södergran, Gösta Ågren and Tua Forsström. Bosley (a poet himself) has translated the Finnish epic *The Kalevala* and selections from the Kanteletar lyrics for Oxford World's Classics, as well as individual volumes of Eino Leino and Aleksis Kivi. He has also brought out with others an excellent volume of translations from Finno-Ugrian oral poetry – a magnificent illustrated book published in English by the Finnish Literature Society, called *The Great Bear*. I have never seen a copy other than my own in Britain, but it's well worth tracking it down.

Finland's poetry has three traditions: an ancient oral tradition in Finnish, and written traditions in both Finnish and Swedish. The two written lines lead rather separate existences. Edith Södergran wrote in Swedish, as did the other poets translated by David McDuff in the Bloodaxe anthology *Ice Around Our Lips* and in the volumes he has translated from individual poets. Keith Bosley covers all three traditions, but perhaps because of the other translations available he gives relatively little of each of the Finland-Swedish poets. There's only one very short poem by the modernist poet Gunnar Björling, said to be "Scandinavia's only Dadaist" – taken apparently from one of his finest collections, the 1933 volume *Sungreen* (though I couldn't find the poem in my volume of *Solgrönt* when I tried to compare the Swedish text). There are only three poems from Claes Andersson's *Poems from the Bottom of the Sea* – short poems which in the original volume work together in bulk to set up an effective atmosphere. (Claes Andersson is also Minister of Culture and a jazz pianist, a precedent for appointing poets to relevant ministerial positions that seems unlikely to have much impact here, alas!)

Bosley gives a wide range from all three traditions, from Mikael Agricola (born in 1510) and the traditional ballad about the killing of Bishop Henry of Uppsala (an Englishman) on a frozen lake in the 1150s, to Pentti Saarikoski and Claes Andersson (both born in 1937). But he doesn't give that large a selection from individual writers in Finnish. He says the anthology was going to be a third bigger but that he reduced it because "I feared that my zeal for being representative might err towards the parochial". I don't know if the reduced size of the anthology was his decision or perhaps that of the publishers but I wish that he had had the confidence to continue with the original project, because he is a fine translator and there is nothing parochial about the works he gives us here. It would have been very welcome to have had more of his translations, to give a wider feel of the writing of the poets included here, and to bring the tradition up to date by including younger writers. It would also have been useful to have biographical notes on the poets, most of whom are not well known here. (There are some notes, but dealing only with specific points that needed clarification.) Finnish poetry has not so

far made the impact in English translation that many other European literatures have had, neither amongst readers nor among poets writing in English. The difficulty of the language is presumably part of the reason, but the number of poetry enthusiasts who speak Czech or Serbian can't be that high, while the work of such poets as Holub and Popa is well-known in translation. No one Finnish poet seems to have caught the imagination here as yet. But perhaps Finland's entry to the European Union will encourage interest in the country and its culture. Finnish is in fact a highly attractive language to hear, and words like "satakieli" – "hundred tongues" – for nightingale seem to me poetic in themselves. But for the moment Finnish readers are better informed about other cultures than we generally are about theirs – they have translations into Finnish by poets like Pentti Saaritsa (born in 1941 and not included in this anthology) whose selections from a wide range of European and other poets has just come out in Finland as *Salaperäinen Seurue* – 'Mysterious Company'.

Skating on the Sea is a very useful anthology, which should make Finnish poetry better known here – it has many fine things to offer us.

THE SONNET HISTORY

JOHN WHITWORTH
CROP-EARED SONNET

Think of things to say and you're Prime Minister. Write them down and you're Shakespeare. Write them down without thinking of them and you're J. H. Prynne. (Larkin to Robert Conquest)

I tend the flame, I tend the sacred flame in Cambridge,
Which is what we tend to doing[1] – our landscape's flat,
Our fens are all the same, they give our Cambridge doves
An *inward* cooing – in common parle, "not everybody's cup
Of tea"[2], caviare to the general[3], *fish eggs!* They scowl
& then screw their puggy noses up, opining "Art" should
"Show its hairy legs!"[4] In corridors of sour officialdom,
Poet-monikers were bruited of late, possibly not J. H.
      Prynne whose time will
      Come. Meanwhile I am
      Content to cultivate
      My garden[5] my fit
      Audience though few[6],
      Which is not you . . .
          Or you . . .
          Or you . . .
          Or you . . .

NOTES
1. R. Graves, *The Greek Myths* (London 1955), 20c, "the fire is so sacred ... it is kindled afresh with the aid of a fire-wheel". This too often a difficult business.
2. The English take tea strong with milk and sugar, a custom frowned on in most civilised countries. In France, a single tea-bag in a pot suffices for up to six people and 'dunking' in the frugal USA means that the same tea-bag can be used many times (cf. the "doggy bag").
3. Shakespeare, *Hamlet* (London 1604) Perhaps a view of caviare with some substance. "Strange meat like blacke sope" (Bullokar 1616). 'He that eateth of Caviare eateth Salt, Dung and Flies' (Moufet & Bennet 1655).
4. J. Crapaud, *L'art Veritable* (Le Touquet 1694), "Helas! L'Art moderne doit demonstrer ses jambes poilus".
5. Voltaire, *Candide* (Geneva 1759), ch 30, 'Cela est bien dit, repondit Candide, mais il faut cultiver notre jardin.'
6. Milton, *Paradise Lost* (2nd Edition, London 1674 Bk VII 1 31. "Though fall'n on evil days... and evil tongues" ib 1 25. Nothing much has changed.

Active Down Under

DAVID WHEATLEY ON THE "HETEROGENEOUS, UNPREDICTABLE AND EYE-OPENING" POETRY OF AUSTRALIA

Landbridge:
Contemporary Australian Poetry

Edited by John Kinsella
Arc, £9.95
ISBN 1 9000 7240 8

FIRST, THAT TITLE: a landbridge is what Australia had to Asia many millennia ago before the continents drifted apart. It's a fitting if optimistic metaphor for the task of bringing Australian poetry to an audience ten thousand watery miles away while we wait for another tectonic heave to knit us all together again. Poetry as geology by other means? "So strange, it might happen!" as Alison Clark puts it in her poem 'Pathetic Fallacy'. One of the strangest things about Australian poetry has always been why people outside that continent don't read more of it, but if the special issues of *Poetry* (Chicago) and *Poetry Review* (edited or co-edited by, yes, John Kinsella) have done anything to create an audience for it, *Landbridge* arrives at an opportune moment.

Given Kinsella's workrate he might easily publish another one before this review appears, but for the moment *Landbridge* is his latest assessment of what is happening in Australian poetry today. It contains short selections from forty-four writers, from canonical elders Peter Porter, Dorothy Hewett and Chris Wallace-Crabbe to relative unknowns in these parts such as Peter Minter, Coral Hull and Sarah Day, though readers of Kinsella's 'Poetry etc' e-mail discussion list will be familiar with some of these. *Landbridge* is arranged alphabetically and doesn't always give its poets' ages, both admirable ways of getting around the usual pressures to map emerging trends or generations. The

> All contributing poets were invited to contribute a short introductory statement, in some cases producing less a stepping stone to the poems than a trip wire. Jennifer Maiden fairly floors herself with "I write to solve the problem of evil", while Les Murray's contribution runs to a laconic three words: "Art is indefensible".

writers were selected, Kinsella explains, as those most likely to make a contribution to Australian poetry in the coming millennium (the first few years of it anyway), which regrettably means the exclusion of the recently deceased Gwen Harwood and Philip Hodgins, among others. All contributing poets were invited to contribute a short introductory statement, in some cases producing less a stepping stone to the poems than a trip wire. Jennifer Maiden fairly floors herself with "I write to solve the problem of evil", while Les Murray's contribution runs to a laconic three words: "Art is indefensible".

Anthology wars in the northern hemisphere are complicated enough, but a number of special factors combine to make an Australian anthologist's job, if anything, even more daunting. For many editors in these islands, the merest "ethnic" presence is enough to prove one's anti-metropolitan credentials (for some editors, it seems, the Irish language simply equals Nuala Ní Dhomhnaill), but obviously in Australia the problem does not admit of such glib solutions. *Landbridge* contains a number of poets of Aboriginal origin, though no translations of poetry written in indigenous languages. The utter remoteness of these languages from Australian poetry in English is not necessarily a bad thing, relieving editors as it does (Kinsella among them) of any illusion that they can represent Australian experience in its totality. Another traditional sticking point in Australian poetry has been the city-bush divide, which Kinsella has spent much of his career attempting to defuse. As against Les Murray's Boeotians and Athenians, Kinsella points out the extent to which the bush, that presumed haven of rural authenticity, has in fact been an urban construct in Australian poetry from at least the time of Charles Harpur and Henry Kendall in the nineteenth century. As Murray himself observes in 'Water-Gardening in an Old Farm Dam': "'Wilderness' says we've lost belief / in human building: our dominance / now so complete that we hide it".

There is nothing unduly surprising in the selections from the best-known poets in *Landbridge*, and it is probably the new voices that readers will be keenest to seek out. As a rule, young Australian writers seem to have far less inhibitions than their Irish or British counterparts about seeing poetry as an extension of their activism in other fields. "I want to tell it like it is, then have something done about it" writes animal rights worker Coral Hull, whose long lines and approach to enjambment are highly distinctive. Murri poet Lionel Fogarty (b. 1959) was the subject of a memorable erratum slip to Peter Porter's *Oxford Book of Modern Australian Verse,* cancelling a premature announcement of his demise. Billed by Kinsella as "the most significant voice to emerge in the latter years of this century", his work does not disappoint even if its gnarled syntax makes it difficult to unpack. Here's a typical passage from 'Biral Biral':

Watching morning asleep
but gunya, sparkling stars windowed at darkness
a giggle swept tears
winning a day and night
no a stomach tight and empty, crawling
search a prey over near grasses
shapes stretched to marvel
the dreaming forced Mum, Nanna and lotta
                                                            people
shouting, me to sing out

Fogarty's suppression of the links in the chain that would make his narratives more immediately graspable is also, most of the time, what gives them their sense of rush and excitement.

Landbridge is dedicated to the memory of John Forbes, who died in 1998. While always having a foot in the door of the various anthologies he has yet to be taken up by a non-Australian publisher. With his fondness for peripatetic "I do this I do that" sort of poems it would be easy in our ignorance to describe him as the Australian Frank O'Hara: he is of course the Australian John Forbes. But he does share with the American a talent for likeable frivolity: who else would interrupt himself at the end of a poem the way he does in 'post-colo-

nial biscuit': "& while I miss the pipeband music / you used to say goodbye with / I love the biscuits in those / plastic ration pacs – they're great!"? Among the poets writing in a post-Forbesian freedom from hang-ups about Australian identity, often in poems about travel and the vagaries of global culture, are Adam Aitken, S. K. Kelen and Laurie Duggan. Further out again on the experimental wing would be Pam Brown, Ken Bolton and Peter Minter.

Satire and wryly comic verse, if not exactly as we understand them up here, can be found in Dorothy Porter and J. S. Harry, while in a more classical way Peter Rose's poems also amuse (his recent *Donatella in Wangaratta* from Hale & Iremonger is worth getting hold of). Lisa Bellear's attempts at satire, by contrast, I found overly sarcastic and self-satisfied. Are white Australian feminists really all as stupid and smug as she describes in 'Women's Liberation'? The way Bellear describes them, it's a wonder we haven't seen Dame Edna in dungarees and flip flops (or 'thongs' as the Australians call them).

A writer who doesn't fit into easily into any category is Philip Salom, whose *New and Selected Poems* from Fremantle Arts Press Ian McMillan endorsed in *Poetry Review* two issues back. An insert box in the collage poem 'The Stone Operas' tells us that "where Paul's severed / head struck the ground /and bounced, there are / now three churches". Not all of Salom is as disorienting as this: he too can be very funny.

Other pleasures along the way include Dorothy Hewett's 'Once I Rode with Clancy'; Peter Goldsworthy's fine sequence 'Chemistry'; Anthony Lawrence's 'A Most Troublesome Possession', a *tour de force* in which he imagines James Dickey flying over Western Australia on a bombing raid during the Korean war; S.K. Kelen's 'House of Rats'; Tracy Ryan's visual trickery in 'Trompe l'oeil'; Joanne Burns's prose poems; and finally, the editor's 'Plumburst' and 'Rat Tunnels in the Wall of the Horse Dam'.

John Kinsella's work on behalf of Australian poetry has been as tireless as it is inspiring. Canada and New Zealand, where are your John Kinsellas spreading the word for you in our insular isles? And where is our John Kinsella, spreading the word for us down under (not that John Kinsella himself hasn't done more than most in this field, in the pages of *Salt*)? Bridges, after all, can carry traffic both ways. Heterogeneous, unpredictable and eye-opening, *Landbridge* sets an impressive precedent for what can be achieved.

An Authentic Air

by Ian McMillan

KATE CLANCHY

Samarkand

Picador, £6.99

ISBN 0 330 37 194 0

YOU'LL HAVE SEEN me recently on buses and trains from Barnsley to Paris and beyond glancing at this book, then staring into space and mumbling as I tried to learn it by heart. I read somewhere that Derek Walcott said you have to learn the whole of literature before you can start to write it, and I've been taking his advice with all the things I've been reading lately, and with this superb book it's been a great help.

Somehow Clanchy's rhythms and phrases imprint themselves on the brain easily, like footprints on wet concrete. I can do the opening poem, 'The Bridge over the Border', without looking. Trust me. "Here, I should surely think of home – / my country and the neat steep town / where I grew up: its banks of cloud, the winds and changing, stagey light, / its bouts of surly, freezing rain, or failing that // the time the train stuck here half an hour". The internal chimes like "changing, stagey", and the cadences of each line, lend themselves to memorability.

What also makes Clanchy's poems imprintable is that they often revolve around an image or an incident that would stay in the mind anyway, even if you weren't taking Derek Walcott's advice. In 'War Poetry' a lesson is interrupted as the class watches a wasp's nest that the caretaker has swept off the roof: "It lies outside, exotic / as a fallen planet, a burst city of the poor; / its newsprint halls, its ashen tiny rooms / all open to the air" and in 'Spell', a lover is imagined: "at your desk, you push aside your work, take down a book, turn to this verse / and read that I kneel there, pressing / my ear where on your chest the muscles / arch...". The poem ends (memorably) "you shall not know which one or us is reading / now, which writing, and which written".

At the stern of the book there's a sequence called 'The New Home Cabaret' (it's the name of a cooker. No, I didn't either.). They're love poems revolving around moving into a new house and although that sounds like a recipe (literally: take two lovers. Take a new house. Mix into a sequence. Redraft for twenty minutes, type in a racy font and send on to a poetry magazine) for disaster, in Kate Clanchy's sure hands it isn't, although these poems are slightly, and I'm not sure why, harder to learn. The cooker makes its appearance in the erotically charged second poem in the sequence: "we shall leave the fifties cooker / grinning where it stands. / It's labelled NewHome Cabaret, / the enamel sink is Leisure: we like / their cool design, bold notes of chrome / and the suggestion of undressing in their aluminium names".

Once the poet and the reader have agreed that everything in this house is significant, then we can get to work. A mirror is an obvious choice:

We're up against the glass, nose
to nose with our doubled selves.

I'm acting as the brace, spread-eagled
over the fireplace.
You're on a chair,
mouth full of screws. We shake
with so much luck and glass, the risk
of arching past ourselves in showers
of shards and ancient memory.

But even a tin-opener reveals its own magic and power: 'The man from Pickford's Movers / has wrapped my tin-opener / (bought from Price Busters /and greased with years of tuna) / in six layers of tissue paper /and a corrugated tube.// On this same principle / were Tutenkhamun's viscera, / liver, kidneys and brains / bottled in four amphorae".

The final poem in the book 'Present', is a manifesto-ish piece about the poet's methods of observation and how she wraps what she sees in significance. It's a fantastic poem, and it's good to try and learn it. I think I've got it. Here's the second verse: "Caught the scarlet-chested builder / spading gravel in the mixer / made him heroic, a war poster; / lent to blazered boys on platforms / blowing smoke rings bright as halos, / the child who trailed her sister / like a slow-to-take-off kite, to the one / hand-fasted couple, their flowered acne / and pram, to all their separate ritual squabbles, an…" Sorry, I've forgotten it. "To all their separate ritual squabbles, an authentic air of idyll". That's it: authentic. That's the word.

Ingredients of Grace

by Gillian Allnutt

MARK ROPER

Catching the Light

Peterloo Poets, £7.95

ISBN 1 871471 65 6

KATIE DONOVAN

Entering the Mare

Bloodaxe Books, £6.95

ISBN 1 85224 429 1

SARAH CORBETT

The Red Wardrobe

Seren, £6.95

ISBN 1 85411 216 3

JANE DRAYCOTT

Prince Rupert's Drop

Oxford University Press, £7.99

ISBN 0 19 288109 4

JEET THAYIL

Apocalypso

Aark Arts, £7.99

ISBN 1 899179 01 1

DONNY O'ROURKE

The Waistband and Other Poems

Polygon, £7.95

ISBN 0 7486 6232 4

MARK ROPER HAS an ear for the funny, quick poetry of speech in both his native North-east England and rural Kilkenny where he lives: "He could take / the tooth out of your mouth with that small bucket" say the neighbours, noting the precision of the digger clearing the ground round an old house ('Breaking Ground'). He also has a tendency to leave the ready-made phrase unravelled. In 'Bawnreigh Slate Quarry' he writes "Here slate is

wiping its own slate clean" and it detracts from earlier lines that depict with fine brevity something of the way Ireland is now:

> Among the lonely minerals and industries
> of Ireland, the quarry's had its day.

You can listen to the loneliness in that.

This is a second collection and there's still an unevenness about the work. Roper will leave a jewel of a phrase without the setting it deserves and needs or allow lovely images to detract from each other by jostling too closely together. In 'To the Comma', reminiscent of early Irish poems and suitably small, he throws away the stupendous "peg for the tents of utterance" by following it at once with "shepherd of phrase and clause". It's terribly wasteful.

Birds bring out the best in this poet, sometimes mediating the mysticism he attempts to take head-on at the end of the collection. 'Red Handed' describes an unsuccessful attempt to let a small bird out of a church. One word tells you it's a country church: "I opened the main door wide. / A bale of warm air fell in". Compactness is all: both the physical-emotional immediacy of the experience – "Entreaty / nerved the air between us" – and the suggested understanding of it are here. As they are in 'Herons' – in close-up not as full of grace as you might have thought:

> Tangled puppet
> you gangled up, a squirt
>
> of fishy piss your final word,
> open to any interpretation.

Gods need distance, as Roper ironically remarks later in the poem. This one has a broken wing and, though the ranger resets it, will not fly again. It dies, but what is buried, beautifully by the poet here, are "all the dried ingredients of grace".

Katie Donovan

Katie Donovan's second collection ends with a poem called 'Gobnait's Shrine'. St Gobnait surely deserves a place in Michèle Roberts' canon of impossible female saints. Above the window of her shrine in Ballyvourney, Co Cork, is a *sheela-na-gig*, a medieval carving of a woman exposing her genitals:

> pilgrim fingers touch her

with sudden intimacy, bare arms
reaching up through the narrow arch
to caress the stone sheela,
whose happy centre is worn away
with rubbing.

Watching this, Donovan can feel "my own parts /
reverentially fondled, praised". Praise the Lord,
then, I say, for the miracle of imagination in a world
where (I quote the back cover) "the female principle is raped, defiled, destroyed and devoured".
'Report' confronts the made-impossible conjunc-
tion of saintliness and sex. Donovan works as a journalist with the *Irish Times* and, as "the first woman
/ to explore the cloister", interviews a young monk
whose humility provokes a decent shame in her:

This is only a morning in my routine,
but with your wide palms
you hold your whole life out to me,
to be shaped by the whim
of my angle.

Her "angle" here is the regret she feels at the loss –
to himself, herself and the world – of his "body, /
meant for nakedness". But there is in the poem no
simple advocacy of sex-as-solution: interestingly, it
is placed after poems on bulimia ('Flush'), silicone
breast implants ('Making Shapes') and pregnancy-
related sickness ('Sick'). It is the body (male/female)
that suffers in our world.

I like 'Report' because its subject is fully realised.
Too often my notes on these poems ask Who?
When? Where? Though I respect the poet's and
journalist's choice to protect her human sources –
to refer throughout the book, for example, to "my
child" (sex, age, name unspecified) – I would have
liked to know whether the guillotine-bound subject
of 'Neck' is girl or woman and when exactly in the
history of Ireland the speaker of 'Strike' is carrying
out his/her hunger strike. After all, a (female) principle can't be raped, defiled, etc: only a person can.

Sarah Corbett

The condition of motherlessness is common to all
who must live in a world made by one male god. If
that condition is earthed in the life of a writer,
through the absence of her mother in early childhood, it can emerge in powerful imagery:

Here are your eyes,
their black centres mimic mine,

dead stars growing
in the sky's fabric;
the inverse of light.

('Inventing My Mother')

That imagery can be beautifully ambivalent:

You are a turned vowel,
the inside of a hole
that sings like the rubbed rim
of a glass.

('Ghost Mother')

You can't get more absent than the inside of a hole.
Yet here is one of the most apt, intimate images of
female sexual pleasure I've ever come across. And
here too may be a description of the state one aims
to achieve in meditation: "the inside of a hole that
sings".

This mother, "always present in [her] absence",
is in that respect not unlike the immanent Christ.
Yet it is not the Christ but the Shaman that appears
in poems such as 'Bird Man', 'Night Flying' – here
a cautious critic would note only that this one is
written in the persona of the heron – and
'Changing':

She is empty and could journey beyond this place,
lifting off like a bird's shadow.

But she remains, rooted and reaching.
I can feel the tender bark of her thighs

In 'Meeting the Alien' there's a description of an
encounter that takes off from the Annunciation:
"You could say an angel came, / a blaze of unnamed
light hitting me... Perhaps they were gods... They
were music resonating / a power like horses...They
left me half-naked in the freezing river".

There is, in this powerful first collection, a willingness, perhaps a compulsion, to set out from the
now familiar world of women's poetry – mother,
grandmother, sister, the housewife, Heloise,
Jocasta, Venus and Co. Like those in her poem
'Pilgrims', Sarah Corbett is embarking on a coura-
geous journey, a journey into other worlds of
"weird":

Kinship dies on the tongue,
its tasted grain shared, diminished,
now a remembered thing.

Jane Draycott

I'm impressed by the cool of Lady Grange whose husband, the Edinburgh judge Lord Grange, had her dumped on St Kilda in 1732. Perhaps panic prompted the poetry in her:

> The tide turns like a regiment for home and I am left
> backstitching the day, brocading the sea for my
> > > bedspread.
> > > ('Lady Grange on St Kilda')

I'm impressed and I'm happy to let the daft lady go down dancing. I'm less happy to leave St Christina – reputed by witnesses to have flown like a bird from her coffin during her own requiem mass in Sint-Truiden, Flanders, 1182 – to her late 20th Century cynicism:

> Up here in the gods where anything goes I am
> > > Lucifer, born
> like a swan from a box, striking the light and
> > > standing well clear
> of the tears
> > > ('Christina the Astonishing')

I find it hard to admire, let alone rejoice in, the mockery of the once-meaningful that Jane Draycott goes in for here and elsewhere in this first collection, though I know how unfashionable I am. The work is technically accomplished and full of energy and the images come tumbling over each other like well-rehearsed clowns – only, for the most part, these poems stand so well clear of the tears that they leave me feeling lonely.

The one that finally opened the door and let me into the collection is called 'Admission'. It may be that senile dementia, even more effectively than death, strips us of our daft credentials. Here is Draycott's mother in the residential home –

> How soon she learned to hide
> in the horseshoe of nodding doll-heads

– and here she is, in 'What matters', recalled in simple snapshots from her and her daughter's life:

> you tying the laces
> on each school day, gripping the shoulders
> of your bike lest it move off alone and leave you

'Braving the Dark' is a long poem written after her brother's death from AIDS at the age of 30. The third part tells of how, "like ambulance-men", they took the piano from his house:

> In one gentle tackle they had the legs
> from under it. Winded, it blurted
> strange harmonies and going down was still.

Jeet Thayil

Jeet Thayil lives in Bombay. Some of the best poems in *Apocalypso*, his first full-length collection, give the impression of having just come to hand, like a drink or a cigarette, in the course of everyday life:

> I scan the headlines, sip from the cup,
> look out at the quiet street.
>
> There it is, all of it
> and it's nothing short of a miracle.
>
> > ('Pushkin Knew Heaven (A Place Where Nothing
> > Ever Happens)')

In 'No More Tears No More' (for Raymond Carver), he goes late and drunk to bed, leaving the silent television on:

> He wakes to rain weeping at the windows.
> In the blue square of light
> a bald man slaps himself in the face.
> "No more tears no more", he says
> in between slaps, this bald man.
> Everything is clear, everything obscure.

If the humour is nicely judged, it comes across as natural. In its mischievousness, self-deprecation, surrealism, it reminds me a bit of Holub.

Thayil searches the global village for subject matter. America exerts a strong pull, giving rise to, among others, a longish poem, 'Other People's Deaths', on the suicides of John Berryman, Delmore Schwarz and Hart Crane – whose life concludes with a "crucial", mouth-watering breakfast "and the waiter thinking, Boy, look at that! / Man's eating like there's no tomorrow."

'Working Girl' belongs to Bombay: "All of Asia is / Captured there in the musk-red exhalations / Of her hair", he writes, then likens her to "a Sumo woman / Sex wrestler". Suddenly, with "I'm thinking of the real thing on TV", we're into an account of wrestling seen on some late-night sports channel from Japan and looking back to see how the transition happened. Best, though, is the irony of this:

she returns
To her place by the door and the thing she knows
Best of all: To love is to wait.

Slyly almost, it brings in another dimension.

Donny O'Rourke

"I belong to Port Glasgow; am a Portonian; a cut below". So O'Rourke establishes his credentials in a foreword to *The Waistband*, his first full-length collection. But he lives in Glasgow now and takes pride and delight in its past and present. "It's 1902", he writes, and

Lake Michigan listens to Clydeside.
In the field of onions, great skyscrapers grow.
Intent on Utopia, they've made Glasgow their
model.
('Second Cities')

And here it is, "frae thi French o Blaise Cendrars", on a starry night:

In this sail snell licht, chitterin, mair nor orra,
Glasca's lik thi jeelit parrymauk o a plant
That kythes againe in its shinners.
('In Thi Warld's Hert')

I quote at my peril, uncomprehendingly. Half a dozen such translations "from the French" are among the swankiest and, I suspect, the funniest pieces here. I could have done with a glossary.

The book could have done with an editor, a dour one, who'd have cut the cackle and put the commas and apostrophes in their places. There's too much self-indulgence, some desperately awful love poetry – though I don't mean the song lyrics included in the collection. It's a pity to swamp the good things – poems on America and American writers and particularly some lovely poems, full of affection, on family.

The poem that will stay with me longest concerns his maternal grandfather, Frank Quigg, who died before O'Rourke was born and is buried in his native Co Antrim:

And so at Ballintoy he lies,
taken at his word, taken from Ballycastle
to this green place where most,
(in sober willing too), he'd wished his stone to stand,
on this adamantine, snaggle shored Antrim land.
('Ballintoy')

A little bit of longing there, I'd say, and a nice end-rhyme.

Spanish Eyes

By John Burnside

DON PATERSON
**The Eyes,
Versions of Machado**
Faber, £7.99
ISBN: 0571 200559

I CAN THINK of two reasons why attempting a translation of Antonio Machado for a British audience would be a difficult and ambitious project. The first, and perhaps most obvious, is that this poet is notoriously hard to translate; his austere yet profoundly lyrical verses tend to slip through the translator's fingers, vanishing on the page when rendered into English, as if, like certain orchids and deep water fish, they can only exist in a very specific habitat. The second reason is less easily pinpointed, but it has to do with sensibilities, with what poets and readers consider important or worth discussing. With the notable exception of Lorca, English readers appear not to have taken to Spanish poetry, with its emphasis on the philosophical lyric, and its concerns with death, solitude and the spiritual path. Machado, in particular, is not an obvious poet to offer an Anglo-Saxon audience. His sensibility is alien to that which dominates English writing; he demands that we set aside the notion that what matters – all that matters – is the social (the public and the personal, as it were) and insinuates the possibility that there really is an inner, asocial, individual soul, in the philosophical or religious sense, a self which is not governed by the laws of the contingent world, but is connected, in some way, to the continuum of being and, surface appearances and worldly distractions notwithstanding, is engaged in a spiritual journey.

Don Paterson confronts both these difficulties head-on in *The Eyes*, a daring and inventive selection of Machado's poetry, rendered into English with astonishing skill and a deep respect (rather than reverence) for the originals. In some ways, it should come as no surprise that his versions of Machado feel so right (right rather than accurate, or correct, as it were – for he is quite prepared to compromise the letter of the text in order to convey the spirit of the poem). Paterson's previous work might have prepared us for the spiritual and lyrical kinship he so obviously shares with Machado, yet his achievement, in *The Eyes*, is one that should not be taken for granted: these are both versions and original poems, in a very real sense, highly inventive solutions, as it were, to a difficult and beautiful problem. So it is that, while readers unfamiliar with Machado in the original can happily read and enjoy this book in the abstract, I fear that Paterson's very significant achievement in recreating the sense world of Machado in a quite alien language might be underestimated, for the time being at least, because Machado's work is still so unfamiliar to us.

Like Lorca, Machado was born in the South (in Seville) but he moved north, and found his spiritual home in Soria, a much harsher, colder city, on the high Castilian plateau. Here he evolved a deeply individual voice, writing lyrics which express, by their very spareness, an austere and exacting spirituality which Paterson recognises as essential to the work:

> The plan, in selecting from Machado's work, was to take a leisurely stroll down the *via negativa*, with Machado as guide, a less bleak route than the brochures describe. The occasional outbreak of negative theology (not to be confused with negative faith) in the written word is characterised by a certain snowblindness, in that it plays – in a way that can be dangerous for the constitution of the poet, and dangerously boring for the reader – far closer to the annihilating light than other poetries.

As much a philosopher as a poet, Machado described poetry as "the essential word in time". He claimed that he was not so much interested in "the word for its phonic value, nor colour, nor line, nor a complex of sensations" as in a "deep palpitation of the spirit". Throughout his life, he was engaged in a refining process, a paring down to essentials, in order to convey this spiritual truth; certain words appear, again and again, in subtly transmuted, almost emblematic form, in his poetry: dream, afternoon, journey, road, time, memory, the familiar. This adds to the translator's difficulties, of course, because words that, in Spanish, carry subtle and powerful resonances can fall flat on an English reader's ear, appearing as clichéd and banal. Paterson recognises these difficulties and, without compromising Machado's intentions or voice, manages to avoid them. His view of the translation process is set out in the introduction to *The Eyes*, and we must be grateful, not only for the poems included here, but also for this brief but highly perceptive essay, which, I would suggest, will become a classic of its kind, just as these versions will come to seem essential to any English reader with an interest in Machado's difficult and rewarding works.

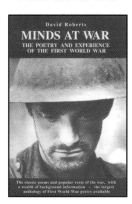

JOHN LATHAM
COMING BACK

You'd recognise the tar-spills
on the railway bridge's stone,
King George's crest
on the cast-iron urinal

you'd know the Swan and Garter,
the oak-tree in the square,
and casting its shadow
over everywhere – the hill.

You'd miss the Friday market
the smithy, Odeon,
Brown's Gentleman's Hatters
replaced by Spud-u-Like

the clock in Main Street
you shinned up in the dark,
advancing tomorrow
by two hours and a half

Catherall the Chemists
– dazzling cut-glass jars,
brass scales in the window
solemn as a schooner –

brook that skirted Ivy Lane,
lazed towards the marsh:
coffined
under forty years of tarmac.

You wouldn't find the woman
who planned a hero's welcome
but had to tell the Silver Band
to change its tune

and gave the cakes and ale away:
who kept those battered boxes
of eggs you blew each Spring,
shouted, yesterday, from coma

"I told you not to play
behind the pumping station",
plunged back one final time,
into the battlefield, to find you.

DIANA HENDRY
DEMON LOVER

Not until someone tells you
he fancies you, do you see
that he's deadly attractive
and wildly promiscuous.
Very soon you're obsessed,
your life not your own,
always wondering when,
he'll seed, spread, touch bone.
You have therapy for infatuation,
the treatment makes you worse.
You try cutting him out of your life
but the cutting hurts. Poison
doesn't work. On some nights
you're wholly in his thrall.
He leaves you, of course –
and for days, weeks, months,
you begin to feel normal.

Then he's back, with that smile,
that dancer's way of metastazing
about your body – almost tenderly.
"I want you, I want you", he moans,
and you can't resist. Somehow
you made him. Now you're his.

K. M. DERSLEY
A PERCH TO SING FROM

I don't get "cosmic"
on the smell of malt and tar
that slides on the water
beneath greasy swans

though down the dockyard
I've seen the men on the boats
letting out the hawser with one hand
and doing something else
with the other.

Yes, I've seen them.

During sleep I'll be walking
without knowing it along the top of some
ridiculous funnel over a grain silo
high up where they grind
that which Cranfield's reduced
exceedingly fine,
walking along there
in sleep suddenly to stumble
on the edge, wake up and
fall out of a dream
promenading on the
lip of Paradise.

I'm not some unexpectedly ennobled
juvenile overweight Byron hobbling
to Harrow and other establishments,
though I once ambled
with hindquarters like
         those of a donkey.

The gutter made its claims
therefore I'm entitled to claim IT
and I reckon "society" fully intends
to keep things that way.

The gutter might have claimed me
but not the stench trap
the drain, but not the lowest part.

ATAR HADARI
FAITHFUL

I have been faithful, after a fashion
your daughter wept and I wept too
when I went to see her in the autumn sunshine
and described how a turned voice, patterned dress, a handkerchief
reminded me of you –

I have been faithful, after a fashion
the girl I met before you died
but never got to tell you of
knows of your headstone
and the places where you lived, alive –

I have been faithful, the foundations
of the building where you lived, the stones
the dank cement blocks in the corner basement
are all counted and commemorated in my heart.

I have been faithful, all the ashes
on your daughter's entrance hall armoire
are in my kitchen, blackening the matches
in the drawer where new girls leave a bra

in the cupboard where I see a smoked glass
in a bottle where I see black tar
in a washing line that holds all of life
in its outer garments I see your smell, your sound

your indentation in the corner caster
chair where friends would come to see you while
your fat cat Mozzie would climb your left shoulder
like a backass parrot – I've been faithful, no-one

sits on the bench outside your house block now –
I have been faithful, now nightly
as in those years, I patrol your neighbourhood
and watch the leaves falling. I watch over your sleeping car.

And in your lobby where the nightly
lights never go out, I wait
for your step in the darkened park.

TIM LIARDET
IN ITALY (BY MATCH-LIGHT)

And I saw what looked like an angel, holding
in his hand the key to the Abyss . . .
Revelation 20:1

Once more he'll get the blob of sulphur to burst
alight, cupped so it will burn up:
see what you can, while you can. See, in

the sudden match's yellow-blue explosion,
your father's features – intent pupils,
nose-bridge, khaki collar and, in each pupil, *flame.*

Because the – *fucking* – kerosene lamp withholds
its merry wick he must read
by the light of matches your mother's insect-scrawl:

see the army tent's sail full of sulphur
sailing him, sailing him
ever further south – flapping and drumming.

On the crease of his brow a mosquito,
a moth's gigantic shadow purring across the page.
And this the last match. Be assured

he'll burn thumb and forefinger, pinched nails,
before he lets the last go out,
so bright. See how the charred stalk dips

against the entrusted dark, the match-wood hissing
to nose fluid forward, yielding to flame.
A while longer light. A while longer.

Every thought of him – like the orange nimbus
itself, or warplans he serves without understanding –
drawn to the sulphur's tear

                        like insects off the river.

DOUGLAS HOUSTON
THE RESIDENT

Three summers here, ten since he died,
Our house, the generous pension gone:
The independence I retain
Is well-rehearsed to coincide
With days whose soft routines go on
Providing care and lessening pain.

Hope's such a personal affair,
Articulated in the light
That's flickering through the maple trees
Above this little garden where
The blossoms of July invite
A sense that age is mostly ease.

At night, in bed, beyond TV,
The past assumes the present tense,
Dimensions open where I find
My photographs smile back at me
And fancied talk can recompense
For fallings short of fair or kind.

With help, I like a walk that leads
Down through the wood, to sit beside
A stream out where this old estate
Gives up appearances to weeds,
Receding acres that provide
A distance thought can imitate,

A prospect past the rusting gate
And roofless shed, a foxgloved tract
Surprised by butterflies, where air
Turns into sky to demonstrate
That endless space is simple fact,
And, heading home, I take my share.

JOHN GREENING
MAGIC

The loss of magic, where did it go, is what
spellbinds me. I was made to look at it,
was invited to touch it, thrust my hand
through it, inspect it briefly from all sides.
It was more real than any mirror-gazing
church service. It pupated from the deaths
of those whose houses were the fairy dells
of the pantomimes they took us to, ogres
transformed to mice, old men to dames, and girls –
all flesh a made-up wonder! It involved
Christmas and countryside and seven planets.
It was hidden in the shellac oyster beds
of school assembly, or in the dog's horn.
When I dug a hole between huge peonies,
through layers of Thames alluvium and clay
I was searching for its source. When I wrote
a story set in the remotest corner
of Chobham Common, I was summoning it.
My father used to do a trick with money:
a coin that vanished would appear wrapped up
inside a nest of boxes. Although I knew
it did not grow on trees – how slow to ripen,
that black-and-white TV! – this was a power
and it could be learnt. An Easter conjuror
performed at primary school, and even when
his Cinderella left a few of her rags,
my friends all jeering in disgust, I saw
prestige in the role. Perhaps this was all
to do with puberty: the thrill of pleasure
in "Colour Change Cords" an escape-rope down
from adult search-lights; the "Vanishing Lady"
a passage to force through beneath high voltage
to the erotic free world. It was not
what I wanted, though I let my future hang
behind its lavish silk, show-stopping, chrome.
Sesame! and my childhood's gone, but magic
beyond the David Nixon show, beyond
the Davenports' magicians' shop, remains
that black magnet in my grandfather's shed,
those black curses in my grandmother's head.

It is as if at unexpected moments,
instead of playing the magician, I
am the tube within the box, black on black
revealing endless streams of paper flowers
to ceaseless patter from a voice outside me.
I should have seen then how it's done: one wishes
to be Illusion, not Illusionist,
to make the things of this world – gold half-hunter,
cigarette case, ring, half-crown, pound-note – vanish
in shadow-play and silent awe, through one's
concealed internal cunning. As they told me
at Christmas, when the latest trick I'd asked for
proved to be some plasticky piece of work
with extensive instructions – *It's the secret*
you're paying for . . .

ANDY CROFT
EDGE

Easy to see why they thought it was flat
    On such a bright and windless day.
This was the view from Mount Ararat,
    The world a perfect circle of grey,
A bright, spinning coin in the palm of the hand
    Contained by the sharp horizon's rim,
    A bucket of sunlight, full to the brim
With all that we know and understand.

Easy too to see why they thought
    This flattened, silver, well-scrubbed flood
Was made for them, each fish they caught
    A salty covenant from God,
Revealed in every rainbow scale,
    A promise that the sea would hold
    The hidden gold with which it's shoaled,
And harvest seas would never fail.

Hard to remember the first surprise
    When the morning was edged by the black silhouettes
Of ravenous long-ships, the fisherman's eyes
    When the round world was caught in his nets,
Violent and strange, too heavy to land,

Too huge to be thrown back over the side,
   An edgeless map, washed up by the tide,
Shaped like a footprint found in the sand.

Easy to see on a day like today
   Why we believe that the world is a sphere,
As the tankers edge their oily way
   Along the slow horizon's frontier
Beyond the curving slope of the earth;
   And why we know we can't disown
   The promise that we're not alone
Painted in rainbow oils on the surf.

Beyond the mirrored edge of all
   We think we understand or know
The unacknowledged monsters crawl
   In the amniotic undertow,
The nightmare, hungry things that creep
   Slowly up the pebbled shores
   Of headlands washed by ocean snores
Where watching cliff-top sentries sleep.

The world's not flat but curved with longing,
   An endless, cambered plain of foam
We whittle smooth by our belonging,
   Ringed by the harbour lights of home,
From where we scan the skies above
   The submerged kingdoms of the blood,
   The unfathomed mountains of the flood
For our returning human loves.

BILLY COLLINS
WAVES

When I was a child in a sunhat
sitting on a beach with a pail and shovel,

I believed that waves began somewhere
on the far side of the ocean,
and whenever one crashed in front of me
spraying my face and making me wince,
I thought it was the end of a long journey
under clouds and open sky

as if every wave were a refugee carrying
a cheap suitcase full of salt water
only to perish in a commotion of shells and foam.

Today I pull into the empty lot
early in the morning,
walk over the cool sand carrying my shoes
and sit down to face the horizon,
to watch the waves that are still coming in,
columns of them collapsing at my feet,
the ancient and the new
all rolled into one billowing fall.

The longer I stay here
the slower they seem to move,
this one rolling in so gradually
it almost stands still like a piece of blue sculpture
and the next one slowing,
then slowing even more, and actually stopping –
something I never saw as a child –

a wave so perfectly motionless
I could wade out and lift it from the sea
then carry it home and place it on a shelf
or hide it inside my mother's black steamer trunk,

maybe give it as a gift to a friend,
a teacher who influenced me,
a beautiful woman who tormented me.
Or I could just toss it back

and let it tumble to shore in the surf,
one of the millions that throw themselves
at us night and day,
under a bright moon or a heavy rain –
another pulse-beat, another vexation,
another throb or surge –
the Eternal, you would say, visiting us
with another unregarded splash
the Infinite tipping its sunhat in our direction.

ELAINE FEINSTEIN
BELLS

Big Ben sounds cold tonight.
Each strike an ache of ice.
My neck feels every gong
as a chill. The traffic halts
and the radio news has
a wartime, childhood voice.

Bong. An honourable war
and simple politics. *Bong*
We sit in the car and absorb
the rhetoric of peace.
And I remember VE day,
jiving with friendly Yanks,

or sitting in the cinema
applauding Russian tanks.
Bong. Dead bodies fill
our telly screen. Who will
suggest a remedy? For God
was not the Commandant

who set up Uncle Jo's Gulag
or sent Emma Lazarus' children off
to napalm gooks across Vietnam.
We did it. *Bong.* The human ape,
inheritor of planet earth, and
from our power there's no escape.

Bursting the Bales

by Rod Mengham

PAUL MULDOON

Hay

Faber & Faber, £7.99
ISBN 0 571 19551 2

THE TITLE POEM to this volume is a deceptively lucid sonnet, in which the speaker bridges the octet and sestet with a sentence epitomizing much of the motivation and method of the book as a whole: "I'm itching to cut the twine, to unpack / that hay-accordion, that hay-concertina". Each of the poems is stratified and compressed, its various strands inextricable not only from each other but from a surprising number of lines found elsewhere in this very substantial and multifarious collection. It is a mixture of different kinds of growth, which all give off the same unmistakeable smell once they have been intertwined and baled ("a bale of lucerne or fescue or alfalfa").

Breaking open the hay calls up memories, some of which are personal, but many of which are shared, borrowed, relayed, coming alive most of all in the retelling. Muldoon's individual memory is interleaved with that of his father, with the folk wisdom of proverbial lore, with the cultural legacy of his own pop music-listening generation, with literary historical echoes of Virgil, and with much more. The settings range from the domestic and familiar to scattered locations as geographically diverse as possible: Ireland, Japan, Australia, Poland, New Jersey. The sonnet is exchanged for the haiku, French for Hebrew, Spenser for Rilke. It is almost as if the most important forms of relating in the book are arrived at on a collision course.

But the mutual communing of these texts is far from undermining the reading process. First impressions might suggest a poetry of short attention-spans, but the opposite is slowly made apparent. The rapid local shifts from one field of reference to another are never merely repeated but frequently revised; they are Pindaric fluctuations that are momentarily distracting while providing hidden accretions of meaning. Muldoon handles the possibilities as if playing a concertina, constantly putting the pressure on and then releasing it, compressing and decompressing, nearly always by running a glissando through musically related phrases and words. This creates a special vigilance in the reader who must learn to distinguish between examples which can take the weight of full meaning and those which can't.

The first person's desire to cut the twine, expressed in 'Hay', is recalled sixty six pages later in the eighth poem of the sequence entitled 'The Bangle (Slight Return)', where Muldoon's father is imagined bending to "unpick the clove- / hitch in the twine with which his manganese-red / suitcase was bound". The enjambing of that hyphenated phrase, joining two lines as the knot joins separate ropes, accentuates the thematic tension between division and connection that this particular sequence and the entire volume obsessively revolve around. A more profound link exists between 'Hay' and a poem about hay-making or, to be strictly accurate, hay-treading, entitled 'Third Epistle to Timothy'. This provides something of an emotional centre to the volume with its compassionate account of work in the fields as experienced by Muldoon's father at the age of eleven in 1923. While its reconvening of material is comparatively restrained, its cross-references are insistent enough to suggest a means of historicizing the kind of poetic hypertext patented by Muldoon. This poetry with a suitcase, bound but always threatening to burst open as easily as the bales in 'Hay', is referentially insecure and restless not because it is postmodern but because it is Northern Irish, in origin at least. It is intertextual because it is intercolonial, its hybridizing a direct response to being identified, even at the age of eleven, with only one of two cultures divided by a connecting language. The New Testament Timothy earned Paul's attention through being especially dutiful, a willing receptacle for the instructions of the Church's great lawgiver. Muldoon's deregulating epistle strikes a distinctly biblical note only at the very end when it paradoxically evokes the very opening of the Bible and the most absolute form of "terra nullius", appealing

to all that spirit-troop
of hay-treaders as far as the eye can see, the coil on
          coil
of hay from which, in the taper's mild uproar,
they float out across the dark face of the earth, an
          earth

without form, and void.

Muldoon's remodelling of the languages of religion and politics is occasionally magisterial but more often impish, the terraforming of an environment in which protocols and formulae of all kinds are repeatedly twisted out of shape, but never so far as to lose their critical elasticity: "A bird in the hand is better than no bread. / To have your cake is to pay Paul. / Make hay while you can still hit the nail on the head. / For want of a nail the sky might fall"

('Symposium').

Robbing Peter to pay Paul, commandeering the language of the Church for the benefit of Paul Muldoon, is a good joke whose glibness reminds us how difficult it remains to discharge the debt to historical uses of language. Rehearsing those uses while simultaneously extemporizing new ones might not prevent the sky falling but we are reminded of its importance, and its importance is safeguarded, by the number of times this particular

Shadows & Cashpoints

by Keith Jebb

J. H. PRYNNE
Poems
Bloodaxe, £12
ISBN 1 85224 492 5

EFFECTIVELY A *COLLECTED Poems*, and his first book with a nationally distributed publisher, this amounts to the moment when Prynne loses a reputation based on not being read, on being the unavailable denizen of mail-order small publishers. This will mean the loss of a certain glamour; a move into economics very apt, for being very reluctant, and for that with a publisher markedly populist in its marketing of poetry (if not in the poetry); a publisher not obviously friendly to the avant garde, and with more of a leaning towards the openly political than to writing whose politics necessitates a questioning of the open, the cut-and-dried.

Turn to the back-cover of the book and blurbs-peak asserts that glamour of Prynne's austere reputation, notably in the first comment: "Britain's leading late Modernist poet". That "late" seems strategic and significant. It substitutes for a "post" we might all be expecting, perhaps to show that Prynne still holds to some techniques of Modernism – but then so do the majority of decidedly post-Modern(ist) British avant-garde poets. Has post-modernity become such a frivolous idea in the public realm that we have to protect our serious writers from it? Does the weight of Prynne's reputation demand the "High Seriousness" of Eliot *et al*, the academicized sterility of what is to be inter-

preted rather than read?

That Prynne could be funny, that he may just be the joker in the pack would appear unthinkable. Yet Ian Patterson, writing in *Poets on Poetry* (ed. Denise Riley, Macmillan), mentions just this fact as "an aspect of Prynne's poetry which is frequently present but hard to pin down".

> I'm slowly waiting for the soup to boil and even the
> slow, pure, infinitely protracted recall of a train-ride
> in northern Ontario (the Essex of north America)
> can't fully divert me from the near prospect of
> Campbell's Cream of Tomato Soup, made I see at
> King's Lynn, Norfolk. Another fine local craft, you
> don't need to believe all you read about the New
> York art industry...
>
> ('Foot and Mouth')

A fairly protracted example, I admit, but characteristic of the earlier work (it is from *The White Stones* of 1969) in that the heavy-handed and decidedly unfunny irony of High Modernism is replaced by a tone of quiet self-mockery. We are no longer above the world, we're in it: the subject is not an anonymous (or in Eliot's term "impersonal") controlling voice, an authority, authorizing a certain form of interpretation (of history, of the writing itself). The subject is a product, a process, in this case of the action of memory and desire (for the soup) commodified but no less sustaining, a desire framed by economics and consumerism.

> and when imitated by
> lazy charade the truth became optional, al-
> ⠀⠀⠀⠀ternative to the grand stability of
> dream: "the transit from drive organisation to cognitive process". The truth has lately been
> welsh & smoke-laden & endlessly local, and
> "getting it right" held the nagging danger of
> not getting it at all. And being right is not so

absolute as being so...

('A New Tax on Counter-Earth')

This is from the 1971 collection, significantly titled *Brass*. *A Note on Metal* (1968), is a short prose essay on the development of value (metal) from substance (stone) from the Bronze Age onwards. It could seem out of place in a volume of poems, unless you begin to understand the history of economics like the history of childhood, as part of the subject's constitutive mythology: or as the last line of 'A New Tax on Counter-Earth' puts it wryly:

The horizon is lit
With the rightness of wayward sentiment, cash
As a principle of nature. And cheap at the price.

A whole essay could be written about his aspect of Prynne's work alone. It is a sort of poetic elaboration of a Marxist theory of subject-production under consumer capitalism. The subject is the bourgeois subject. It cannot be anything else, and if the truth seems proletarian – "Welsh & smoke-laden & endlessly local" (some allusion to Raymond Williams, the Welsh Marxist critic of Cambridge University of the 60s & 70s?) – this has to be measured against the difference between "being right" and "being so".

Is this revolutionary? Yes it is. Not with a manifesto's authority, of course, since what it does is present our memories and desires as a reflex of a system, the "I" we hold so dear as a choosing being as being defined by the limits of its choice. Capitalism relies (and always will) upon the illusion of autonomy. So Prynne takes the lyric, the most autonomous and I-centred of the arts and turns it inside out, like a glove. It's uncomfortable because many of its most insightful statements ("cash as a principle of nature") sound oxymoronic. Also funny. If you get a chance, compare this to John Ashbery's use of "we" as a principal pronoun, and his drift towards an expansive, discursive poetry.

Prynne's poetry gets if anything more difficult through the seventies and eighties. The "I" which used to organise the vast range of discourses the writing includes slips to the side. More and more the writing addresses a "you". In *The Oval Window* (1983) this "you" is placed in its alienated life-experience – "So what you do is enslaved non-stop / to perdition of sense by leakage / into cycle: one man's meat / better late than never" – in which the act of reading and the act of surviving become strangely conjoined. Information becomes less of an issue; issuing becomes a form, short pieces which seem to begin after the beginning, so we play catch-up:

You're flat out?
But the method sorts downwards, wired up
From the NCR cashpoint; you must choose the order
of choice, on the nail from which the shadows hang.

The discontinuities in the work are often haunting: the nearness of cashpoint and shadows, placing us in a world where emotions do not transcend the banalities of existence. And what if these things are banal only because we cannot formulate their place in our emotional complexities? The traditional lyric poet's skills had much to do with bringing unlike and like together in metaphor. "My love is like a red red rose". Then Gertrude Stein wrote "a rose is a rose is a rose" and kind of levelled the field. Her writing was based on repetition and the accumulation of tiny shifts of difference, metonymic rather than metaphoric. So her medium was prose. So what do we do with a poet who uses lyric with a metonymist's skill? When the juxtapositions are often so violent, when the very tradition of the lyric seems to have been violated? Obviously many people will find this book unreadable, unconsumable, like some product where we cannot tell the wrapper from the thing it wraps, or where we can't get the bloody cellophane off, anyway. I'd suggest a kind of trust. Prynne, the poet, the informing intelligence in these poems (Prynne as a defining trademark for these writings, no more or less) is humanity and humour, and sometimes just to grasp the working stuff, can be a start at least. Sometimes the more difficult the work the quicker one should read it, so you don't try to make it fit the patterns you project.

A blow to the side of the mouth
strike harder, it is important
to be lyrical and joyous
then again, another
on the neck, how can this
be done so strongly without
the highest fidelity,...

(from *Word Order*, 1989)

I have developed a deep respect for this poetry, for what it does. Also for its place in a continuing tradition of writing in this country, poetry that challenges settled notions above the place of writing and its construction in the world; and it is in the context of names such as Tom Raworth, Maggie O'Sullivan, Wendy Mulford, Allen Fisher, and dozens more, that any evaluation of Prynne's reputation must take place, diverse as all these writers are. But we are no doubt going to be asked: "Is he better than Heaney?" by people who are outraged at the very thought that he might be. My answer comes from the pen of Ernest Fenollosa, write of *The Chinese Written Character as a Medium for Poetry* (c. 1906): "A ring tailed lemur is not a constitutional assembly".

The Stitches Show

by Carol Rumens

CIARAN CARSON

The Ballad of HMS Belfast

Picador, £6.99
ISBN 0 330 373 69 2

The Twelfth of Never

Picador, £6.99
ISBN 0 330 373 70 6

THE LEADING NORTHERN Irish Catholic poets of the post-Heaney generation are intensely concerned with language. In different ways, the poetry of Ciaran Carson, Paul Muldoon and Medbh McGuckian submits English poetic form to the pressure of a submerged linguistic identity. They are Irish writers for whom English, even if, literally, the poet's "first" language, is a necessarily complex inheritance. It must be questioned, stretched, rendered more allusive, layered with arcane reference and never simply taken on trust. If such writing expresses linguistic disenfranchisement, it does so with such immensely self-confident and sophisticated verbal dexterity that the whole notion of disenfranchisement becomes ironical. These poets are super-stylists, playing English poetry brilliantly at its own game, checking the referee and sometimes executing complex passes among themselves for their own private satisfaction.

Before the 1987 publication of *The Irish for No*, Carson was a quiet, solid worker in the groves of Heaney. But at that point he rebelled into language, set free by a rangy "long line" that has been attributed variously to the influence of C. K. Williams, Louis MacNeice and traditional music. He became a raconteur-poet, giving, in bravura poems like 'Dresden' and 'Judgement,' artistic method to the rambling and round-about narrative techniques of the popular story-teller. In the same collection he also devised a short form consisting of one five-line and one four-line verse, a suitably asymmetric structure from which to simultaneously unleash and contain vivid portraits and anecdotes of his native Belfast. The most located of poets, he was now able to zoom in on his location and highlight its fractures, material, linguistic. These nine-liners relish the nitty-gritty of the real world, even as it shatters under the onslaught of "Belfast confetti" or Belfast irony, and as inner-city development, as well as internecine madness, combine to cause the "linen backing" of his childhood on the Falls Road to fall apart. The various symbols that keep the collection itself tightly cohesive – chalk, tobacco, MacNeicean snow and roses, *et al* – are never merely symbolic, and language not just linguistic philosophy but inky print and alphabets.

From the *Belfast Confetti* collection on, the preoccupation with linguistic matters intensified, as book-titles alone imply: *First Language, Opera, et cetera*. But, at around the same time, Carson diversified into full-scale prose-writing, producing two dazzling tapestries of personal and local history in *Last Night's Fun* and *The Star Factory*. So was Carson's rangy, rackety, friendly Falls Road of a "line" always aspiring to true fulfillment in prose, and is now to be considered obsolete? We shall have to wait and see. Meanwhile, it can be revisited and savoured in *The Ballad of HMS Belfast* which, as the book's subtitle, 'A Compendium of Belfast Poems', suggests, forms a kind of 'Selected', bustling but coherent. Elsewhere, in collections of his new work, Carson concentrates his formidable verbal energies on the 12-syllable alexandrine, a metre which seems to provide an ideal "reign", rhythmically supple, neither too slack nor too tight. You could hardly call *The Alexandrine Plan* (Gallery, 1998) a mere run-up to *The Twelfth of Never*; the earlier work, a trilogy of brilliantly realise translations of Rimbaud, Baudelaire and Mallarmé, declares the form already to be second nature to Carson. What he achieves in the original alexandrine poems that make up the new collection, is the cross-pollination of the sonnet with the tall story – the sung, rather than spoken, story, perhaps. The result is a scintillating contemporary picaresque, a linked narrative of symbol-spangled adventures in Other Worlds: contemporary Japan, Celtic myth, the Napoleonic Wars, various "Irelands" and altered states both nineties-sinister and sixties-delicious.

Slipping folksong themes and figures into this bricolage, Carson reminds us that linguistic virtuosity in Ireland lies not only in the demesne of the literary giant, of Joyce or Flann O'Brien, but in the "hungry hills" of Anon. An ancient ballad, 'The Song of Lies', begins:

> T'was a comical sight that I saw by the roadside,
> An eel with the pipes, and he playing a broadside,
> The trout with fine shoes in the pool by the heather,
> And the sheep cutting turf in the black winter
> > weather.
> (Translated from the Irish by Donal O'Sullivan).

Carson's opening sonnet 'Tib's Eve' (a term that, as his note explains, symbolises "never"), recalls the above nonsense-verse as well as reminding us of a favourite fancy-tickling trope of story-tellers the world over: "Once upon a time there was and there was not...". But innocent playfulness can be deeply subversive and 'Tib's Eve' begins with a line mischievously plucked from a sentimental Anglican hymn:

> There is a green hill far away
> Where cows have longer horns than any that we
> > know;
> Where daylight hours behold a moon of indigo
> And fairy cobblers operate without an awl.

So our tour begins with an Irishman's ironical glance across the water as he anchors in the unconquerable place in which "ghostly galleons plough the shady Woods of True" (a neat reversal of Marianne Moore's "real toads in imaginary gardens"). Does this mean that *The Twelfth of Never* is really all about poetry and music? Well, it is and it isn't. Astute readers will have fun spotting the quotes, the literary references, the folksong titles and the guest appearances (is that blameless Seamus at target-practise over there? Is Miss Dickinson

dancing with Professor Muldoon?) But serious bloodstained history seeps into almost all the poems. A war between red and green is raging. Symbols dangerously mutate: "Poppy the emblem of Peace and the Opium Wars", "Poppy the amber of Death and the Special Powers". The poppy is perhaps the most obsessively juggled image in the book, a reflection of its enormous political potency in both the North and the Republic of Ireland. In the corruscation of red and green, blue and amber, you could spot Wilde's carnation, the severed hand of the gruesome Ulster legend, dragoons and rebels and Red Branch knights, Bloody Marys and shamrocks (the latter may be blue), a coin of Spanish gold, nettle-green eyes and cyanosed lips: all these and more turning up in unexpected places. Carson's vocabulary, like his syntax, refuses to be constrained by current useage: colourful archaisms such as *tattersall, dandiprat, thimblerig, picketpock, pinking*, add wonderfully to the texture of sounds. 'Trooping the Colours' contains a gorgeous list of the costumes and colours of war, with a final grim meditation on what happens to them, a tribute, possibly, to that virtuoso poet of lists and war-elegies, Michael Longley:

> Breeches, gaiters, busbies, turnbacks, epaulettes and
> > plumes;
> Dolmans, girdles, cloaks of tiger-skin, valises;
> Jackets, waistcoats, frocks, the fruit of many looms;
> Bicorns, sashes, shakos, piping, braid, pelisses-
> Carmine, pike-grey, crab-red, drab, philemot-yellow;
> > (Etc.)

One of the marvels of the collection is its intertextuality. The sonnet is a form that invites closure, and, for a narrative poem, a cadence every fourteen lines could be fatal. Carson circumnavigates the risks by constantly picking up threads – symbols and lines, key-words and phrases, so that seventy-seven distinct poems also work as a symphonic whole. 'Patchwork', an earlier, Belfast poem about granny's handsewn quilt, comes to mind, especially her comment: "The stitches show in everything I've made". This of course implies a self-criticism, but, as the grandson-poet knows, sometimes the stitches are part of the beauty of the design. Nothing comes unstitched in Carson's magnum opus, except, I'm sorry to say, the actual pages of these volumes. My copy of *The Ballad of HMS Belfast* has already shed leaves and *The Twelfth of Never* is threatening to do so. Nice jackets, Picador: shame about the glue.

THE CLASSIC POEM

SELECTED BY PHILIP GROSS

A CONFESSION: THE first time I happened on Rilke's Tenth Elegy I was, as they'd say now, gutted. A couple of years earlier I'd co-authored a book, *The Air Mines Of Mistila*, with Sylvia Kantaris – a world that evolved itself between us as we wrote, as near to automatic writing as I've ever come. And there in his country of Laments (isn't the German word *Klage* untranslatable, in its sound?) was our landscape, our tone... Except it wasn't ours now; it was Rilke's. There's the test for a writer: you find "your" thought in an earlier poem; are you pleased? Thumbs up for the thought, thumbs down for the ego.

And if anything merits the word *classic*, Rilke's elegies do. The extracts below are just a glimpse of one in the cycle of ten for which he waited, with famous patience, seven barren years. It is a grand project of massive authenticity – unashamedly a vision – that affirms life and death and suffering and joy. Because joy and life are easy to affirm, it can look as if Rilke harps on about their opposites, but no, this isn't a sermon on the spiritual value of suffering. He is celebrating one organic whole. Maybe it is even harder to grasp that now, at the end of a century of therapies and healthcare and all kind of striving towards quality-of-life, than it was in 1922. I'm still struggling with it. Sometimes I find it profound, sometimes morbid, sometimes erotic, sometimes Buddhist, ecstatic or glum. But always a challenge, in our age of unambitious ironies. Call the *Elegies* a monument of late Romanticism if you like, the kind of vision only laughable New Agers fall for, or point out the more repellent aspects of their author's personality... yes, but they won't go away. And isn't that what *classic* means?

RAINER MARIA RILKE

FROM *THE DUINO ELEGIES*: THE TENTH ELEGY

But how alien, alas, are the streets of the city of grief,
where, in the false silence formed of continual uproar,
the figure cast from the mold of emptiness stoutly
swaggers: the gilded noise, the bursting memorial.
Oh how completely an angel would stamp out their market of solace,
bounded by the church with its ready-made consolations:
clean and disenchanted and shut as a post-office on Sunday.
Farther out, though, the city's edges are curling with carnival.
Swings of freedom! Divers and jugglers of zeal!
And the shooting-gallery's targets of prettified happiness,
which jump and kick back with a tinny sound
when hit by some better marksman . . .

. . . Oh, but a little farther,
beyond the last of the billboards, plastered with signs for "Deathless",
that bitter beer which seems so sweet to its drinkers
as long as they chew fresh distractions in between sips . . .,
just in back of the billboard, just behind, the view becomes real.
Children are playing, and lovers are holding hands, to the side,
solemnly in the meagre grass, and dogs are doing what is natural.
The young man is drawn on, farther; perhaps he is in love with a young
Lament . . .   He comes out behind her, into the meadows. She says:
– It's a long walk. We live way out there . . .

[. . .]

But there, in the valley, where they live, one of the elder Laments
answers the youth when he questions her: – Long ago,
she says, we Laments were a powerful race. Our forefathers worked
the mines, up there in the mountain-range; sometimes even
among men you can find a polished nugget of primal grief
or a chunk of petrified rage from the slag of an ancient volcano.
Yes, that came from up there. We used to be rich. –

And gently she guides him through the vast landscape of Lament,
shows him the pillars of the temples, and the ruined walls
of those castles from which, long ago, the princes of Lament
wisely ruled the land. Shows him the tall
trees of tears and the fields of blossoming grief
(the living know it just as a mild green shrub);
shows him the herds of sorrow, grazing, – and sometimes
a startled bird, flying low through their upward gaze,
far away trace the image of its solitary cry. –

Translated from the German by Stephen Mitchell

Reprinted by permission of Picador from *Selected Poetry of Rainer Maria Rilke*,
translated by Stephen Mitchell.

Like Fruit in a Bowl

by Jane Holland

SHEENAGH PUGH

Stonelight

Seren, £7.95
ISBN 1 85411 243 0

SOPHIE HANNAH

Leaving and Leaving You

Carcanet, £6.95
ISBN 1 85754 407 2

TOBIAS HILL

Zoo

OUP, £6.99
ISBN 0 19 288102 7

FERGUS ALLEN

Mrs Power Looks Over the Bay

Faber, £7.99
ISBN 0 571 20029 x

STONELIGHT IS SHEENAGH Pugh's ninth collection, and her experience shows. In 'Envying Owen Beattie' – where the body of arctic explorer, John Torrington, is discovered under permafrost – Pugh gives this detailed account a poignant Sleeping Beauty spin, which won her the 1998 Forward Prize for Best Individual Poem:

to feel the lashes prickle
your cheek; to be that close
to the parted lips:

you would know all the fairy-tales
spoke true: how could you not try
to wake him with a kiss?

However, this prize-winning poem throws up some interesting questions about Pugh's handling of form. 'Envying Owen Beattie', like many of the poems in *Stonelight*, is peppered with what I feel to be intrusive punctuation: commas, colons and semi-colons abound, the lines above being a fairly

typical example. Reading these poems aloud, however, I was often unable to see how to depunctuate them without radically altering the physical shape of the poem. Being of the opinion that the poem on the page needs to work harder than the poem in performance – that poetry which is not purely oral asks form to reflect tone and pitch for the silent reader – I found Pugh's approach clumsy and aesthetically off-putting. Yet in the title poem about stones, here being skimmed across water, Pugh demonstrates a sure-footed sense of rhythmic anomalies which refuse to be tied down to any set line or stanza length:

The eye flinches. When they sink,
if they sink, the light they left

wells out, spills, seeds itself, prickling
like stars, on a field that never takes
the same shape twice.

This "field that never takes / the same shape twice" is surely poetry, and the fact that Pugh describes the stars of inspiration as "prickling" rather than shining may explain her over-use of punctuation. This is a poetry that prides itself on being lyrical in tone, yet is deliberately unpredictable in its rhythms, a pleasing combination that keeps the reader both guessing and reading. When she attempts humour or a "contemporary" note – for instance, in 'Lovesong', 'Graffiti Man', 'Aardvark' or 'The Tormented Censor' – I found the result either twee or heavy-handed, making me feel that Pugh's strengths lie more in lyrical narrative than in a day-to-day observation of modern life.

But there is a poet for every taste, and while Sophie Hannah's third collection, *Leaving and Leaving You*, is also not something I would leap into the nearest bookshop for, I must concede that she is very talented in her chosen discipline. The ironic formalism of her first two collections, *The Hero and the Girl Next Door* and *Hotels Like Houses*, assured her of a place amongst the foremost of our "light verse" poets, and this latest offering seems unlikely to shake that position. But there is more to Hannah than so-called "light verse"; her work is steadily moving beyond the limitations of that tradition and closer to a voice which recalls Dorothy Parker's bitter-sweet satire, though possibly without that poet's daring or sureness of touch. 'Steven's Side' cynically explores the cliché of the woman who supports her man, in all senses of the word:

I am supporting Steven.
I am at Steven's feet.
    I put him first and even
give him a thing to beat.
    I put him first and even
then he will not compete.

Here, a telling pun on "beat" is concealed by the insistent repetition, song lyric-style, of phrases which lull an audience into hearing their humour, rather than their underlying seriousness. Unlike Parker's notoriously sharp closures, the stinger has been buried.

But if this is "light verse", is "light" intended to imply lightweight, superficial, for entertainment purposes only? If so, Hannah's work rarely fits that description. On the contrary, she is a poet steadily working towards a redefinition of the genre in which she has most naturally found herself. Her humour is typically anarchic, and her best titles read like cryptic crossword clues: 'She Has Established Title', 'His First If Lady Only Just', 'Over and Elm and I'. As social, and predominantly feminist satire, this poetry works. To dismiss it simply because it does not pretend to lyricism would be short-sighted of me. But I do have gripes with some of these poems, moments where the phrasing is downright clumsy, though it's hard to demonstrate this with brief quotations:

    ...if the sort
of woman who believes her hopes and ears

predominates over the doubting kind
in your portfolio...
                                    ('Your Darlings')

To my mind, this is a case of abstract generalisations taking the place of much-needed particulars. I don't want to hear about his portfolio, I want to actually see it. Indeed, when Hannah turns her hand to metaphor and simile, I find her poems far more accessible, as in 'The Burning Scheme' with its "Moon like an orange in a sea of gin". For Sophie Hannah's work to really appeal, I would have to see far more accurately observed detail in that vein, balancing urban-style anecdote with a sense of nature's continuity.

One poet whose work positively drips with the accurate observation of nature is Tobias Hill in his latest collection, *Zoo*, where a reputation for urban lyricism is reinforced by these well-crafted and ambitious new poems.

Hill's voice is already very much his own, nor does he need to raise it in order to be heard. But the influences of Armitage, Hughes and Heaney seem to be present: a taste for understatement; anecdotal writing; the closeup detail taken directly from nature, then skewed through ninety degrees to give the reader something completely new, even unique. So in 'Drunk Autumn Midnight below Victoria Embankment', "the mud is thick as meat" alongside "the broken fingerbones / of clay pipes", while in 'Dowsing with Whalebones', the poet leaves the labyrinthine city with "a souvenir of pigeon feathers / the colour of magnet".

The desire to tell a story – and to present it simply, *á la* Armitage – is also evident in many opening lines: "In the small hours / we eat sushi with our fingers" ('Sushi'), "We're waiting for the lights to change / and you are reading borrowed books" ('Leonardo's Machines'), "After work he feeds the wolves / in Regent's Park" ('Doctor Crippen in Love'). But once the magic territory has been opened up, Hill moves swiftly into his own idiom, looking at caged animals, considering sights, smells and sounds in minute detail, and working in a painterly fashion with colours, white and green in particular. I rarely bother with ridiculous statistics, but the regularity with which these two colours crop up intrigues me: twenty-four instances of "green" and twenty-one of "white", in a short collection of only twenty-nine poems. Many poems actually revolve around these colours, like the white fog of 'Closing Time', and the hills of 'The Island of Pumpkins', "their green bowls cupped / against green bowls".

It would be easy to dismiss these repetitions as a tendency towards simplistic over-qualification. But I believe that Hill is attempting to come at the essence of an experience through a symbolic use of colour, drenching this otherwise urban collection with primitive light and nature: white and green. With this third collection, Hill promises to be a real force in poetry, displaying an utterly contemporary understanding of how nature continues to work its strange and powerful influence, even in a predominantly urban landscape.

Fergus Allen in *Mrs Power Looks Over the Bay*, is another poet who refuses to allow contemporary poetry to become hard-edged and purely anecdotal. He demonstrates an unrelenting fascination with people and the places they inhabit, often dwelling on the Irish in a way that feels both modern and bizarrely Edwardian at the same time. The influence of Joyce may be at work here, with a poem like 'Parental Guidance' possibly recalling those torturously respectable boarding houses in Dubliners, where, after a night of "half-suppressed squeals" heard through a hotel wall, a child is surprised to note how

> Moustached Mr Ganly in his striped shirt
> Was genial over the porridge and haddock,
> And Mrs G spoke mildly of the weather
> As she brushed crumbs off her flowery blouse.

The humour here is unmistakable, as is the sense of being an outsider, an observer, someone always just passing through.

Allen is at his best when speaking through another character, looking back with nostalgia and often regret at an imagined time, as in the title poem where Mrs Power's casual lyricism is saturated with an almost political irony:

> Oh I've come a long way
> with your father since our skins first touched
> like fruit in a bowl.

This gentle wave-like rhythm is typical of Allen's work. In his easy formality, these poems exude an awareness that urban realities may push aside the past if it is not laboriously pieced together with "the familiar twinges / of rapport no sooner made than broken. // Perhaps not made at all". ('Odyssey') Dense with implications, this complex collection is working hard to retrieve what it can from poetry, so that after reading them, I often felt like Allen's 'Fishers of Fish' did after casting their lines, where "Minutes later we hauled them in / with creatures hooked up from the dark beneath".

Soul of Poetic Wit

By Peter Forbes

Short and Sweet: 101 very short poems
Ed. Simon Armitage
Faber, £4.99
ISBN 0 571 20001 X

101 Sonnets from Shakespeare to Heaney
Ed. Don Paterson
Faber, £4.99
ISBN 0 571 19732 9

VERY SHORT MEANS less than 14 lines, and that includes a lot of wonderful poetry especially if its chosen by someone like Armitage who has a refreshingly open response to what he finds. Some of these poems have been Poems on the Underground and most could be. There are the poems that hover around a lyrical moment, epitomised by MacNeice's 'The Brandy Glass', squibs like Carol Ann Duffy's 'Mrs Darwin', epigrammatic wisdom like Auden's 'Epitaph on Tyrant', comic grotesques like Ian Hamilton 'Finlay's Catch'. The book has a cleverly contrived fade-out with the poems getting shorter and shorter, via Gavin Ewart's one liner 'The clanking and wanking of her majesty's prisons', and Edwin Morgan's 'Siesta of a Hungarian Snake', and meets its apotheosis on Don Paterson's Zen mountain with the master failing to turn up.

The innovations in sonnet writing in this century have given Don Paterson a wonderful field to play in. You can tell he relished it from his introduction, which is one of the best tracts on writing verse I know. Paterson blows one of poetry's great trade secrets when he says: "The truth is most poets work to a stricter or a looser formal template, one sympathetic to the rough shape of the poem they have in their heads, then go *nose blows rose chose Montrose suppose Atholl Brose comatose* for days on end until something in them goes *Bingo!* And they hit the right combination of music and sense". There are some discoveries here: e.g. Edna St Vincent Millais 'I Being born a woman and distressed' with its pungent post-coital summing up: "...Let me make it plain: / I find this frenzy insufficient reason / For conversation when we meet again".

Neither Grainy Nor Sandy

By Peter Forbes

WISŁAWA SZYMBORSKA
Poems New and Collected 1957–1997
translated by Stanisław Barańczak and Clare Cavanagh
Faber, £14.99
ISBN 0 571 19668 3

NOT ALWAYS FAMED for the judiciousness of its choices, the Nobel Literature Committee's selection of Szymborska, near the end of the century, was a master stroke, for she has some claim to be seen as the representative poet of the late 20th century. As she says in her Nobel Prize address, included here, she has rarely pronounced upon poetry, just kept writing some of the most wry and unillusioned but also sprightly poems of the age. You can gauge something of the quality of her poetic sensibility by the fact that Ecclesiastes and Joseph Brodsky are the only poets she cites in that introduction.

Ecclesiastes' long look comes naturally to her – she continually debunks human pretensions and human certainties – "Poets if they're genuine must also repeat 'I don't know'" – but she she's quite a few notches up the scale of human optimism from Ecclesiastes.

Parable became a habitual mode of thinking in Eastern Europe under communism. A poet would wake up every day and what she saw was the world translating itself into sardonic fables. A Ted Hughes would hammer a stone to make its atoms ring but Szymborska interrogates it like this:

I hear you have great empty halls inside you
Unseen, their beauty in vain,
Soundless, not echoing anyone's steps.

Aspects of life rarely noticed by poets are central to her work. Others poets will raid the myth kitty, seize some minor history and weave their mythology around it. Instead Szymborska notes that there are already too many such stories: "Our stockpile of antiquity grows constantly, / it's overflowing". What should we do with all the stories pullulating and proliferating around us? Traditionally poets are guardians of the collective memory but Szymborska notes the impossibility of rescuing much of existence from oblivion:

What should we give them? What do they need?
...
We three billion judges
Have problems of our own,
inarticulate rabble,
Railroad stations, bleachers, protests and processions,
Vast numbers of remote streets, floors, and walls...

The sheer plurality of the world constantly torments Szymborska: "So much world all at once – how it rustles and bustles! / Moraines and morays and morasses and mussels..." She is drawn to try to make sense of all the stories that lie beyond the little circles of family, friends and acquaintances. The random way people are implicated in history is an obsession, as in 'The Terrorist, he is Watching' in which she details the comings and goings of people in the minutes before a bomb explodes, the man who was walking out but then goes back in because he's forgotten his gloves, the girl who was obscured by a passing bus and it's not certain if she went in or not ("we'll see when they carry them out").

Szymborska's vision is the antithesis of Blake's. She gathers up the things of this world and shows how empty they are when we are not there to invest them with meaning. In 'View with a Grain of Sand' she recounts the ancient Greek atomist's view of things: instead of seeing heaven in a grain of sand she insists that to itself the thing isn't even grainy or sandy – to me an essential precondition of seeing the world aright:

The window has a wonderful view of a lake,
But the view doesn't view itself.
It exist in this world
Colorless, shapeless,
Soundless, odorless, and painless.

This volume adds 64 poems to the 100 published as *View with a Grain of Sand* (1996). The translations were obviously done with a real love for the originals, and this is the kind of poetry that doesn't get lost in the process. Michael Hofmann has said "I can't imagine anyone not enjoying Szymborska", and he's right: here is a poet you can safely recommend to anyone without the usual poetic health warning.

A book in the knapsack for the new Millennium.

PENELOPE SHUTTLE
IN HIDING

Just as a dowser
Despite the hole in his fortune,

knows where the finest water lives,
and why it needs so much depth,

aqua de plus belle,
so I remember you

passing for rain
in your orchard,

amid your lakes in flight,
your lapinière of light,

your usable marvels:
beginning again and again,

but hidden as water hides,
in its modest science,

until found, or unfound,
as the world on its travels

wills.

NEWS/COMMENT

FORWARD

The Forward Prizes will be announced as usual on National Poetry Day. The shortlist for the Main £10,000 Prize is: Kate Clanchy, *Samarkand;* Jane Draycott, *Prince Rupert's Drop*; Carol Ann Duffy, *The World's Wife*; Paul Muldoon, *Hay;* Jo Shapcott, *My Life Asleep*. For the £5000 first collection prize: Matthew Caley, *Thirst*; Amanda Dalton, *How to Disappear*; Nick Drake, *The Man in the White Suit*; Christopher North, *A Mesh of Wires*; Christiania Whitehead, *The Garden of Slender Trust*. For the Best Single Poem in a magazine, newspaper or competition: Caroline Carver, 'Horse under Water'; Robert Crawford, 'Zero'; Robert Minhinnick, 'Twenty Five Laments for Iraq'; George Szirtes, 'Backwaters: Norfolk Fields'; R S Thomas, 'Blackbird'.

CORRECTION

In Pete Morgan's poem, 'Good Orts' (*PR*, Vol 89 No2, 1999), there were two errors in the last two lines. The poem should end:

> ...the broken bell
> which clangs one off-key on the earth
> cluttered with smithers of good orts
> to wink their thousand eyes at rain.

We apologise to Pete Morgan and to readers for the errors.

ALDEBURGH FESTIVAL

The 11th Aldeburgh Poetry Festival is relaxing its non-returning rule, which means that James Berry, Sujata Bhatt, Maura Dooley, Brendan Kennelly, Sheenagh Pugh and Carole Satyamurti will be there. There is the usual impressive international contingent, spearheaded this year by the Romanian Ana Blandiana and the American Billy Collins. The latter has a British debut book coming from Picador next year; meanwhile you can find him on page 44 of this issue.

Friday 5 November
Workshops with Michael Laskey, Glyn Wright, Billy Collins, Sarah Maguire, Tamar Yoseloff
James Berry 6pm
Readings: Sujata Bhatt, Michael Donaghy, Michael Laskey, 8pm

Saturday 6 November
Maura Dooley, Carole Satyamurti, Tamar Yoseloff, 10.30am
Kate Bingham, Sheenagh Pugh, 2.30pm
Jamie McKendrick on Seamus Heaney, 4.30pm
James Berry, Sarah Maguire, Robin Robertson, 7pm
Sunday 7 November
Masterclass with Michael Donaghy, 10.15am
John Hegley, 1pm
Ana Blandiana, Billy Collins, Peter Jay, Brendan Kennelly, 3pm
Box Office: 01728 453543

NET VERSE

Perhaps it could only happen in America: *Gumball Poetry* is a literary journal that publishes not only on the web, but also by putting poetry and art into gumball machines. Their site at **http://gumballpoetry.com** not only hosts the journal itself, but also describes the project, and tells you where their machines are. As a way of distributing poetry, this must be one of the most imaginative around.

I don't usually have many good words for usenet poetry newsgroups, but one that might be worth looking into if you're after workshop style comments and criticism is **alt.arts.poetry. comments**. The atmosphere is (mostly) friendly and constructive, though it's a busy group, so be prepared for several hundred messages a day if you sign up. Guidelines and more information are on the group's home page at **http://www.go-get.co. uk/gopoems/aapc/**

If it's magazines rather than books you're after, try the guide to the UK's independent press at **http://www.little-magazines.co.uk/** for its addresses and submission information. It seems fairly comprehensive, though the rather idiosyncratic layout may confuse and irritate some.

Finally, there's some good stuff going on at Steve Duffy's "debris" site at **http://www.debris.demon. co.uk/** where he has a variety of innovative dynamic and hypertext poetry, as well as some more conventional material. Some of it is browser-specific, though, and will only work with Internet Explorer. Don't miss 'The Thing' – an interactive piece that allows the visitor to construct poems by selecting lines.

Send other useful or interesting things to me at **peter@hphoward.demon.co.uk**

LETTERS

NOT TRAD

Dear Peter,

Andrew Motion has had quite enough flak thrown at him recently without an invented bit being added to the barrage. In her interview with the new Poet Laureate (Vol 89 No 2, p.4), Jane Hardy confidently (and provocatively) says: "Anthony Thwaite describes your poetry as 'traditionalist'" – a judgement Andrew Motion rightly rejects. I challenge Jane Hardy to quote any passage in which I described Motion's poetry as "traditionalist". It isn't a word I much use, I don't believe it of Motion's poetry, and I can't believe I ever said it.

Yours sincerely,

ANTHONY THWAITE

Low Tharston

Norfolk

BRIAN JONES FACTS

Dear Peter Forbes,

Peter Bland's enthusiastic essay about the poetic career of the shamefully underrated Brian Jones (Vol 89 No 2, p.52) was welcome and long-overdue. While I and many admirers of Brian Jones would take issue with Bland in preferring his later politicised, discursive style for his earlier, highly-charged lyrics, this was a valuable overview of a writer whose best work can easily stand comparison with that of much more fêted contemporary poets like Douglas Dunn, Andrew Motion or Carol Ann Duffy. However, the piece was marred – as many positive overviews often are – by irksome basic errors regarding publication details and dates. For the record, then, Brian Jones has produced the following mature collections in these (precise) years: *Poems* (London Magazine Editions, 1966), *A Family Album* (LM Editions, 1968), *Interior* (Alan Ross, 1969), *Poems & A Family Album* (LM Editions, 1972), *For Mad Mary* (LM Editions, 1974), *The Island Normal* (Carcanet, 1980), *The Children of Separation* (Carcanet, 1985) and *Freeborn John* (Carcanet, 1990).

Yours sincerely,

TERRY KELLY

Jarrow

POBOOKS ONLINE

Dear Peter,

In the current issue of *Poetry Review* (Vol 89 No 2, p.95) I was disappointed to see that your roundup of poetry bookselling websites didn't mention the PBS's website through which we recruit members and sell books (at discounts of up to 25% to members) online via secure credit card encryption facilities.

While holding a zillionth of the stock Amazon lay claim to, we do supply post 1950 books from every poetry publishers in the UK and Ireland and offer titles which have gone through our well respected selection procedure. The catalogue is about to undergo an expansion whereby we will supply full backlists from all publishers, not just those books we consider to be the best of each quarter, and we may extend back to include the first half of this century. Our postage charges are based on the actual cost to us, so it is still usually cheaper overall to buy books from us.

Yours sincerely

CLAIRE BROWN

Director

PBS

SOME CONTRIBUTORS

Peter Bland's *Selected Poems* were published this year.
John Burnside's latest collection is *A Normal Skin* (Cape).
Harry Clifton's prose book, *On the Spine of Italy*, was published by Macmillan this year.
Kwame Dawes' new collection, *Mid-Land*, will be published by Peepal Tree Press next year.
Elaine Feinstein's new collection, *Gold,* is due from Carcanet next year.
Rita Ann Higgins' new collection, *They Always get Curried Chips*, is forthcoming from Bloodaxe.
Kevan Johnson is a former Assistant Editor of *Poetry Review*.
James Lasdun's latest book is *The Siege*, Random House.
Jayanta Mahapatra is one of India's leading poets.
Rod Mengham is Director of Studies in English at Jesus College, Cambridge.
Roberto Mussapi has translated several volumes of Seamus Heaney's poetry into Italian.
Peter Redgrove's latest collection is *Orchard End* (Stride).
Carol Rumens' collection of Irish poems, *holding pattern*, was published by Blackstaff last year.
Ian Sansom is writing a study of Auden.
Robert Saxton's first collection, *The Promise Clinic*, is published by Enitharmon.
Penelope Shuttle's *Selected Poems* are published by OUP.
Carole Satyamurti's *Selected Poems* are published by OUP.
Fred Voss's second collection, *Carnegie Hall with Tin Walls*, was published by Bloodaxe in 1998.
David Wheatley's first collection is *Thirst* (Gallery).